CW00743120

OLICANA'S CHILDREN

For Jean, Nick and Caroline

First published 2009

IGS Publications
Ilkley Grammar School
Ilkley, West Yorkshire.
www.ilkleygs.ngfl.ac.uk

© Peter Wood 2009

The right of Peter Wood to be identified as the author of this work has been asserted in accordance with the Copyrights, Designs and Patents Act 1988.

All rights reserved. No part of this publication may be reproduced, stored in or introduced into a retrieval system, or transmitted in any form, or by any means (electronic, mechanical, photocopying, recording or otherwise) without the prior written permission of the copyright holder and publisher.

A CIP catalogue record for this book is available from the British Library.

ISBN 978-0-9562123-0-6

Printed and bound by Leeds University Press

All proceeds from the sale of this book are for the benefit of Ilkley Grammar School

OLICANA'S CHILDREN

Ilkley Grammar School
1607 – 2007

SAPIENTIÂ ET STATURÂ PROFICIAMUS

Peter Wood

Floruit, Floret, Floreat,

Olicana's children cry,

Through good or ill,

God guard thee still,

Our boast through years gone by.

Chorus of the School Hymn.

Contents

Preface

2007 heralded our 400th anniversary. Not many state schools can boast such a long and proud tradition of education in their local community.

Times change, people move on, educational initiatives come and go. We may be in the twenty first century, yet I hope our traditional values hold true, and that these, wedded to innovation, will continue to see Ilkley Grammar School thrive in the next 400 years.

Headship is a great privilege. To be Head of Ilkley Grammar School is even more so. The fact that so many students remember their school so fondly and so frequently entrust their own children and grandchildren to us, speaks volumes. Schools are people not buildings (thankfully perhaps, given the challenges of some of ours!) and our students remain our greatest asset. This book is as much a testament to every one of them since 1607 as it is a history.

I am especially indebted to Peter Wood, firstly, for taking on the formidable task of compiling and collating all the material, and secondly, for making it so readable. I certainly feel very proud to feature here!

Gillian James
Headteacher

Introduction and Acknowledgements

This book originated in a conversation I had with Gillian James in April 2007. A suggestion that, for the four hundredth anniversary, I might write something about the School's recent history took on a life of its own, and, before I knew it, I had agreed to write about the entire four hundred years. Much of it has been a fascinating journey of discovery. It has certainly taken longer than the few months I notionally set aside and has led me into corners I didn't know existed.

The idea that this was a story of seamless development, onward and ever upward, was swiftly dispelled. The beginnings were distinctly unpromising; there is not even any certainty that it was the founder's intention to set up a school at all. For the first thirty years it had no building and it was only saved by a further legacy seventy years later. In the nineteenth century it declined to a point where, for twenty years, though it had a board of governors, it had neither building nor pupils. In 1893 it re-opened on Cowpasture Road as a very different school and was almost bankrupt within four years when the governors ordered an extension they could scarcely afford. It has gone through countless transformations, reflecting changing social, educational and political priorities. It has been a village school, an endowed school with boarders, an all-boys and then a mixed selective grammar school, a 13-18 comprehensive upper school, an 11-18 secondary and a specialist school. For almost two hundred and fifty years it existed in a single room. Since the early 1890s it has endured five major building programmes on a difficult site. It has been administered by a Board of Trustees, by the Charity Commissioners, by the West Riding, by Bradford LEA and by Education Bradford. Thus it has never lacked challenges, yet it has always seemed able to draw strength from them, to adapt and develop to meet the needs of the times. This book attempts to tell the story of the people who made all that possible and of the pupils who benefited from it.

Much of it, inevitably, is drawn from the school archive. I am indebted to all those who, over the years, have ensured that such material has been preserved, particularly to Elizabeth Howard who has spent many hours organising it and to the late Norman Salmon who, through his own research, added greatly to the store of knowledge and who wrote the first 'History' in 1957. My thanks are also due to Tony Barringer for allowing me to use some of the anecdotes in his 'A Century At School' and for reading the manuscript. I am indebted to Mike Dixon, for his helpful advice, for the account of Parson Fenton, the description and print of the Cowpastures, and the photo of the Wilkinson memorial brass. Margaret Chambers, Derek Hyatt, Elizabeth Howard, Angela Hughes, Marjorie Jackman, Ivan Minto, Will Varley and Mary Weatherall have all provided me with their own recollections. Lt. Colonel H.V. Dawson kindly allowed me to use some of the earliest documents associated with the School. I am grateful to the Churchwardens of Ilkley Parish Church for permission to use the illustration of the Watkinson brass and to Ben Rhydding Methodist Church for permission to illustrate the Wilkinson memorial. My thanks to Margaret and Denis Warwick for their helpful suggestions and for information about the Burley schools and to Mike Burke, Archivist of Ashville College, and Harrogate historian Malcolm Neasam for their advice. The staff of the West Yorkshire Archive Service in Leeds and in Bradford and the staff of Ilkley Library have been unfailingly helpful. I am grateful to Gillian James and to Sue Pawson for their encouragement, to Cathy Russell and Fiona Hogg for their publishing skills, to Kathy Fuller for reading the proofs and to John Moss for the cover design. Finally I must apologise to all those who have played an important part in the story of the school but whose names, due to the constraints of space and time, I have been unable to include.

A particular concern in writing this 'History' was that my own part in the story, as Headteacher from 1979 to 2002, might conflict with my role as author. I have tried to minimise any latent autobiographical tendencies by using relevant documents wherever possible.

I am especially grateful to my wife Jean, who not only encouraged me and read the manuscript but who had once again to admit Ilkley Grammar School into our life at a time when she imagined such intrusions were long past.

Peter Wood
March 2009

Some Godly and Charitable Use

In 2007 Ilkley Grammar School was four hundred years old. A successful specialist school, with over fifteen hundred students and a rich tradition of serving the town and its neighbouring villages, it was justifiably proud of its achievement. It celebrated in style. There were articles in the local press, reunions of former pupils, archive displays, a Thanksgiving Service, an Anniversary Ball, a visit by the Princess Royal and even a specially-written musical. Yet had things turned out differently four hundred years earlier, as they might well have done, none of this would have happened. Indeed this very public celebration was all a far cry from the murky events which, as the seventeenth century drew to its close, had combined to produce a school for those children living in the cluster of houses which centred on Ilkley church.

The Manor Court records present a vivid picture of life in the village at that time. There was a pinfold where stray animals were held; villagers were fined for breaking it and it had to be kept in regular repair. Boundaries were beaten each year. You could be fined for eating flesh in Lent, for allowing unlawful games in your house, for "casting carrion in the water", for cutting green wood for your bow. The men of Wheatley had to scour their ditches, John Longfellow had to "putt awaye his dogge before Mawdlenmas", scolds were condemned to the ducking stool. It was ordered that "every husbandman in Ilkley in his due course shall take the towne bull into ther custody and meate him well in winter time." Pigs wandered about. Archery butts were still standing. The "little loin" between Wheatley and Ilkley, the forerunner of Little Lane, was so impassable that people could scarcely get to church. Assaults were common; the vicar was even fined on one occasion.

One of the village's more prosperous men, George Marshall, died around 1598 and it is thanks to his legacy that Ilkley Grammar School was founded. Yet that tells only part of the story. We can't even be sure that it was Ilkley's first school. Schools were often attached to chantry endowments and we know that in 1474 William Middleton established a chantry, dedicated to St Nicholas, within Ilkley church. Chantries were endowed by pious benefactors and a priest was appointed to pray for the soul of the founder and other named persons, and in many cases to teach a school. When chantries were closed by Edward VI in 1547 some schools also closed, but, if the keeping of a school was laid down as a duty of the chantry priest, it was often allowed to continue and this may have been the case in Ilkley. The Ilkley chantry was relatively wealthy, for around 1500 William's son, Nicholas Middleton, endowed it with extensive lands in the area of the present Brook Street and between Cowpasture Road and Leeds Road. In May 1551 the chantry lands were granted by the King to the twelve Governors of Sedbergh School. Known henceforth as the "Sedbergh Lands", they included "le Cow Leaze" and "le Cow Close". Over three hundred years later, in 1881, it was from the Governors of Sedbergh that the Governors of Ilkley Grammar School purchased five acres of these lands, which then became the site of the present school on Cowpasture Road. It is, incidentally, from the chantry and the "Sedbergh Lands" that the modern Chantry and Sedbergh road names in Ilkley are derived.

Whether or not a chantry school existed, we do know that, almost thirty years later, Ilkley had a schoolmaster, though his status is unclear. Queen Elizabeth and her Privy Council were at

A nineteenth century drawing of Hollin Hall, home of Thomas Maude. Rebuilt in 1623, it has associations with both the Maude and Heber families.

From Collyer and Turner: 'Old Ilkley'.

pains to ensure that the religious beliefs of such men were beyond reproach and it was left to the bishop or his representative to verify this. Thus, according to the Parish Documents of the Diocese of York, an inspection was carried out in 1575 by George Slater, Chaplain to the Archbishop. He records that in Ilkley there was a schoolmaster, Constantine Harrison, "non admodum eruditus qui tamen juniores commode docere queat" ("not very learned but nevertheless sufficiently able to teach the younger children"). It is hardly a ringing endorsement and Harrison is not heard of again.

By the late 1590s, when George Marshall died, some in Ilkley may well have felt the lack of a properly-established school. We know very little about Marshall. He was living in Ilkley in 1589, when he was summoned before the Manor Court and fined 3s 4d for a rescue from the Bailiff, in uncertain circumstances, of "a maide of Parish Wieff daughter." He was a relatively wealthy man who had made his money by lending sums at interest on good security and he left a substantial estate of £466 13s 4d. From this he directed that the not inconsiderable sum of £100 should "be employed to some godly and charitable use." There is no copy of the will and we can only deduce what it said from later documents. There isn't even any evidence that Marshall ever intended his money to be used specifically for a school or a schoolmaster. His executors were Thomas Maude, George Snell (the Vicar), John Lodge and John Waite and they simply decided that this was how he had wished the bequest to be employed. It was a momentous decision but they then made the serious mistake of giving all the money and the responsibility to Thomas Maude. The Maude family had lived in Ilkley for over two hundred years. Thomas, who lived at Hollin Hall, was patron of the living, had appointed George Snell and was altogether a prosperous man. In the event, rather than investing the money, he simply pocketed it and made an informal agreement to pay the schoolmaster, William Lobley, £10 a year. It was soon realised that the whole arrangement was vague and unsatisfactory and that in any case there could be a major problem when he died, because the £100 might simply be swallowed up in his estate and lost.

Unease over the situation caused the executors to fall out among themselves and particularly with Maude, who seems to have been a slippery character. One quarrel is graphically recounted by John Cromack, "a husbandman, about 60 years", who had known George Marshall and gave evidence later in the dispute. He recalled:

> About five years ago there was some difference amongst George Marshall's executors about paying the schoolmaster

his wage, and then Mr Christopher Middleton came to George Snell's house and was something angry with the said Thomas Maude, and they talked together at the backside almost an hour, after which they returned into Snell's house and said they were agreed, and Christopher Middleton willed the said Thomas to recite their agreement, who said he would make up a £100, and that Lobley, the schoolmaster, should go to Baron Savile to let him know he would refund the £100 given by George Marshall. Thomas Maude promised to lay it in land paying £10 a year.

The verdict of 27th September 1603. It is signed by Sir Thomas Fairfax, Sir Mauger Vavasour, Christopher Bainton and John Metcalfe.

West Yorkshire Archive Service (WYL639/363)
By Courtesy of Lieutenant Colonel H. V. Dawson.

Maude clearly felt he could make personal use of the money for on another occasion, according to the deposition of John Brearey, he "borrowed of John Waite and George Snell £10 of school money, paying the interest to them in Wm. Janson's house in the presence of John Lodge and William Day."

The disunity among the executors and in particular their mistrust of Thomas Maude led them, on 30th September 1602, to submit the whole matter to arbitration by Christopher Bainton and John Metcalfe of Ilkley with Sir Thomas Fairfax of Denton and Sir Mauger Vavasour of Weston as umpires, binding themselves in the sum of £80 to accept the verdict. These gentlemen decreed, on 27th September 1603, in an impressive document carrying their signatures and seals, that the original £100 had indeed been intended for the maintenance of a schoolmaster and a grammar school and that it should be used for that purpose henceforth. Any of the Marshall legacy held by any of the executors was to be paid to William Middleton of Stockhill and Anthony Maude of Helthwayt Hill by 10th May 1604.

That should have been the end of the matter but it was not. Thomas Maude died soon afterwards, and when in 1606 the schoolmaster, William Lobley, died, still owed a year and a half's salary, Waite had to bring another legal action. He must have been persistent, for he was not a wealthy man and the lawsuit went on for some time "utterly impoverishing him." Eventually, on 25th May 1607, the final, decisive award was made. Fairfax and Vavasour ordered that all litigation between the executors should cease. They re-stated the position with total clarity:

> We do order and award that the said sum of one hundred pounds so given by the said testator shall for ever hereafter be employed towards the maintenance of a Schoolmaster of a Grammar School at Ilkley aforesaid for teaching Scholars there."

They made clear their view that the original legacy had been paid to Thomas Maude by his fellow executors with this intent. Maude's executor, Anthony Maude, was told that he must, by 29th September, pay Fairfax and Vavasour £100 "with the intent that it shall be put out to use at the rate of £10 yearly towards the maintenance of a schoolmaster for ever." The schoolmaster was to be appointed by the Archbishop of York, together with Fairfax and Vavasour or their heirs and was normally to be the Vicar of Ilkley, "if he shall be thought and taken by them to be fit and capable of the said place." Thus was established a link between Church and School which was to continue unbroken until 1872. The heirs of William Lobley were paid £15 for salary arrears. It was a long award with many additional clauses and it needed

The document of 25th May 1607 which finally determined that George Marshall's £100 "shall forever hereafter be employed towards the maintenance of a Schoolmaster at Ilkley for teaching Scholars there." Signed by Sir Thomas Fairfax and Sir Mauger Vavasour, it is, in effect, the foundation charter of the School.

West Yorkshire Archive Service (WYL639/364)
By Courtesy of Lieutenant Colonel H. V. Dawson.

another petition from John Waite to Lord Sheffield, Lord President of the Council of the North, before Anthony Maude, under the threat of legal action, finally accepted it and undertook to hand over the money. It was, as Norman Salmon says, "the nearest thing to a charter that the old school ever possessed."

So Ilkley eventually had its school on a proper, permanent, legal basis. It had been a difficult birth but 25th May 1607 is the accepted date for the foundation of Ilkley Grammar School.

The School Where I Got My Learning

There was now a school but there was no building. Teaching simply took place in the church, which cannot have been a satisfactory arrangement. It wasn't helped by the Marshall family who, by 1634, had moved to Idle and Shipley, in the process appropriating £52 of the school's money. It required a binding order on John, Hugh and Nathaniel Marshall and Lawrence Lawson, who were told to pay it back "at Denton Hall, within the County of York between the hours of six o'clock in the forenoon and four in the afternoon on the 8th Day of October next coming" for the money to be recovered. Meanwhile frustration over the lack of a school building was coming to a head. A meeting was called on 2nd January 1635 which drew up a document stating that "by general consent of the inhabitants of the parish of Ilkley aforesaid, we whose names are here subscribed do undertake to pay our proportionable rates towards the erection of a school house." There were fourteen signatories, five of whom had to make their mark. No time was lost. By 11th April 1637 the Grammar School is referred to as "now lately erected and built in Ilkley." The chosen site was on land probably owned by one of the fourteen, Christopher Bainton of Wheatley, on the road to Addingham just along from the church, and there the building stands to this day. Nikolaus Pevsner says it is "no more than a cottage with a middle doorway and two four-light windows" but it was to serve the town as its school for well over two hundred years.

Without more financial backing the Grammar School would not have survived. George Marshall's original endowment had been worth £100 in 1607. The 1635 document notes that "by a late and unavoidable casualty the sum of money given to that charitable use is impaired." It had declined to £89 and was put into the hands of Reginald Heber and Christopher Bainton, "by them to be improved until (by the interest thereof) the sum be made up to one hundred pounds." Payment was subject to negotiation: "Such of the parishioners as send their children to the school should pay such sums as they and the schoolmaster shall agree upon."

The original bequest continued to decrease in value throughout the rest of the century. The problem was that it was never invested in land; it simply remained as money. Fortunately Heber's son,

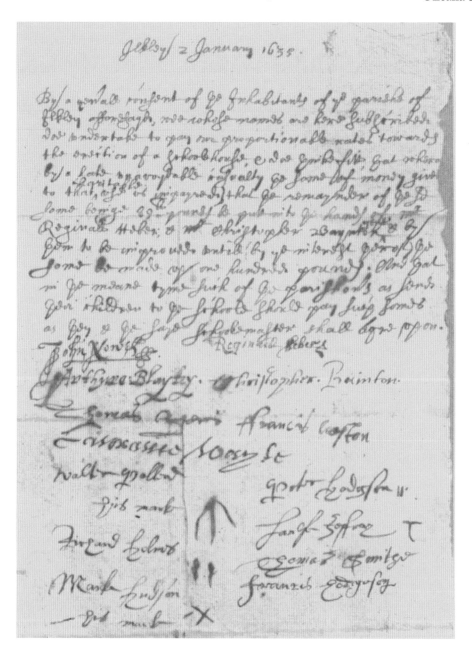

The document headed "Ilkley 2 January 1635" which records the agreement of fourteen Ilkley men to pay for the building of the original Grammar School on Skipton Road.

It is signed by (first row): John Howell, Arthur Blaykey, Thomas Rogers, Laurence Wayte, Walter Pollard (his mark), Richard Holmes (his mark), Mark Hudson (his mark) and (second row): Reginald Heber, Christopher Bainton, Francis Beeston, Peter Hodgson (his mark), James Jeffray (his mark), Thomas Smith, Francis Hodgeson.

West Yorkshire Archive Service (WYL639/368)
By Courtesy of Lieutenant Colonel H.V. Dawson

another Reginald and a former pupil, made a second bequest in July 1696. Perhaps remembering the muddle over Marshall's money, and with the trained mind of a lawyer, he made his intentions in his will crystal clear. He left £100 to the Church and, "to the school where I got my learning," a further £100 "to be likewise laid out in land to the intent that the Schoolmaster for the time being may receive the interest and benefit thereof." This, together with other money added to Marshall's bequest, enabled the Trustees to invest a total of £256 1s 6d in fifty four acres of land with farm buildings, comprising Taylor's Farm, Collyer's Farm and Wade's Farm, at Bewerley, near Pateley Bridge in Nidderdale. The estates were conveyed in August 1701 to the School Trustees, Wilfred Lawson, Richard Witton, John Heber, Edward Bolling, William Currer, Peter Parkinson and Thomas Bartlett, and the Churchwardens of Ilkley "upon trust to apply the rents and profits to the joint use of the vicar and the schoolmaster in proportion to the sums above mentioned." It was provided by the Deed of Trust that the schoolmaster "do and shall teach and instruct all the male children gratis which shall come to be taught and instructed by him." Henceforth the Church was due to 2/5 of the rents and the School, essentially for payment of the schoolmaster and other necessary expenses, was due to 3/5. This all worked well as long as the vicar was the schoolmaster but when, later in the century, the roles became separated, it eventually led to a great deal of trouble. More importantly, this investment put the School on a sound financial footing and was to have a crucial part to play in ensuring its continuation as a grammar school at a much later date.

We don't know a great deal about the School at this time. English and Latin were, it seems, the basis of the curriculum. Depending on the schoolmaster, Greek and even Hebrew might be added. It was, it seems, well-known in the area; one of its old boys, William Lyster, writes of it as "this famouse schoole" and, at the peak of its reputation, it certainly helped prepare the sons of gentlemen for university and the professions – Heber himself became a Lawyer of the Inner Temple. In an early record of building maintenance, two shillings and eight pence was paid in 1691 for mossing the back of the schoolhouse and five pence for the moss. There was trouble in 1710 when the Vicar, George Dawson, who was also paid as the Schoolmaster, took the payment "and hath been requested to teach English, but said he would not, and if forced to it would teach it at an end, and they should have beating enough." This was clearly unsatisfactory and the Trustees complained, "It is not reasonable that the parishioners should lose the benefit of their Children's learning of English for 8 years, and that Mr Dawson should take the profits and teach no English at all." Dawson was ordered to comply with the provisions of Heber's will. A decree of 26th January 1711 made it clear that if he or any succeeding vicar failed to do so, the Trustees would withhold payment and ensure it was given to someone who was prepared to teach.

It seems Ilkley had some trouble with its vicars, for in 1758 people complained to the Archbishop of York about the Revd Edmund Beeston, a local man, who "now is and always hath been since he was elected master of the said school very careless and negligent in the performing of his duty as a Teacher, for which reason the greatest part of our children have got but little and no education, and the salary of our said school is had and taken in as if there had been no neglect at all." The Revd Beeston received a ringing endorsement from the Archbishop, who had "full confidence of your discharging your Duty not only as a good Schoolmaster, but as a good subject to the King." In his reply the Vicar was at pains to underline his suitability as Schoolmaster: "The Classicks have furthermore been one of my favourite studies, of my proficiency in which, and also of my Temper, Industry and Diligence, I could have procured the most ample testimonies had his Grace required it."

There was also financial trouble. In 1770 the original £100 was lent by the curate, George Benson, to Joseph Pollard of Fairweather Green, the Schoolmaster and a descendant of Walter Pollard, one of the fourteen signatories. Pollard promised to repay it on 15th January 1771. The interest of £4 10s per year continued to be paid but, remarkably, everyone seems to have forgotten about the loan. Eventually, almost thirty years later, the Trustees of the School Estate discovered what had happened and, fortunately, were able to call in the money.

They had not learned their lesson. In the early years of the nineteenth century Mr Wilson of Manor House, Otley, had cause to examine the school documents, found that the same thing had happened again and reported to the Trustees:

It appears that the £100 has, in 1799, been lent to Beanlands the present Master upon his own bond only, though land security had been given for a preceding Master [presumably Pollard]. This Beanlands may be a very responsible man but, to a stranger, the presumption is not much in favour of the property of a village schoolmaster and who, should the money be lost, the Trustees may, eventually, have some trouble about the deficiency. Inquiries should be cautiously made about these matters, if a more satisfactory security be, if possible, obtained. 'Tis a bad plan to let the Master have the money at all.

The Trustees seem once again to have been disconcertingly lax in recovering the money. Only when Beanlands died in 1818 did the Vicar, William Holdsworth, write to Sir William Vavasour at Weston Hall, "I am expecting every day to be informed that Mr Beanlands' executors will pay in the hundred pounds belonging to Ilkley School." It is with a sense of relief that he is able to write on the following day, "I duly received yesterday the Bond securing payment from the late Thos. Beanlands to the Trustees of Ilkley School and I will take care to settle the business as soon as I am called upon."

In spite of such setbacks, the Grammar School continued to serve the community on into the nineteenth century. It was essentially a village school controlled by the vicar who, from the late eighteenth century, often employed an assistant as schoolmaster. The Revd Holdsworth's letter to the Trustees about the appointment of Beanlands' successor shows how he went about his work:

In answer to your letter, dated March 28th, I beg leave to observe that it has been my wish ever since Mr Beanlands died to obtain a Person well qualified to teach Reading, Writing and Arithmetic – the salary, to the present time, has been very small, but the Trustees of Mr Heber's charity let the Estate to fresh tenants this Candlemas, and now the Income will be upwards of £70 a year; an advertisement was put in the Leeds Mercury a fortnight ago, and we pitched upon the Schoolmaster at Burley last Thursday but only gave him his answer yesterday. We have been anxious to get a person who has been accustomed to teach. Mr Gill is well recommended indeed, but the Person appointed has always been thought superior ever since he applied. I hope the School will be carried on so as to give satisfaction to the Town and Parish.

In 1829 the Brougham Commission was set up to inquire into the Charities in England and Wales and its brief observations on "Ilkley Endowed School – Marshall's and Heber's Charities" constitute the first official report on the School. Having recorded its history and property it continues:

The Vicar holds the appointment of master of the school, but the scholars are taught by an assistant. The school has long been conducted on the footing of an English-school only, and all the children in the place are admitted on application to the vicar or the assistant, and they are taught reading without any charge, and writing and accounts on the payment of a small weekly sum. The average number of scholars is about forty. The trustees pay to the vicar out of the rents of the estates £46 17s 4d a year, and to the assistant £70 a year, and they retain the remainder of the income for the reparation of the school-room, which is a very old building.

In 1830 William Holdsworth died. Since, at the same time, there was a vacancy for the post of Schoolmaster and the new Vicar, Joseph Clarke, did not live in the parish, the Archbishop of York and Sir William Vavasour, under the terms of the 1607 award, intervened and appointed to the post the Curate, George Fenton. Whether or not he made a good schoolmaster is not recorded but Robert Collyer, the Ilkley blacksmith who went on to become a celebrated New York preacher, has left a singular description of 'Parson Fenton':

He would shave on a Sunday morning, and, as he was going to the church, had been known to tell the butcher to send up a fine leg of mutton. He also had the curious gift of shedding tears in all sorts of unexpected places while he was preaching, and this was a great marvel to the rustic mind. He told his congregation one piping hot Sunday in the cholera year that he had lost or forgotten his sermon, and would dismiss them with the benediction, saying with a lovely look of confidence, "It is no use preaching when you have no sermon. And now etc..." The madcaps under age looked for some such rare fortune again, but did not get it.

The varied requirements of the School are illustrated in the account book. On one day, December 6th 1842, Messrs. England were paid £5 16s "for new desk, forms and repairs at the school", William Parrott was paid 17s 6d for "windows, pointing and repairs" and James Pickles was paid £3 5s "for glazing and painting." More intriguingly, on December 22nd 1843 T. and W. England were paid 6s "for wood and work for desk and hat pins for Ilkley School."

Eventually there was more trouble about money. Under the terms of the conveyance of 1701 the vicar was the schoolmaster and, as the schoolmaster, he was due to the 3/5 of the revenue from the Bewerley lands which attached to the School. In practice, however, he employed someone else to do the job at a lower salary. Two employed by Mr Snowdon, who became Vicar in 1842, were Mr Hobson, known as 'Knocking Johnny' on account of his knock-knees, and his successor, Thomas Wood, who appears on the famous photo of the old school. Matters came to a head in 1863. The Bewerley rents were £105 10s 10d. 3/5 of this,

£63 6s 6d was given to the Vicar but it was pointed out that, in accepting it and not passing it all on to the Schoolmaster, he was taking part of what should have been the Schoolmaster's salary. Such was the strength of feeling that by 1864 angry parishioners had got up a petition which they sent to the Charity Commissioners. They complained, "The charity connected with the Free Grammar School in this place gives to the Vicar, the Revd John Snowdon, the yearly salary of about £65; but being unable to undertake the duty himself, he, at a less salary, employs a person to do the duties of Schoolmaster in his place but seldom visits the school. From inefficiency arising from this arrangement, the children derive little or no benefit from the Charity." Clearly the temptation to appoint a cheap master was doing nothing to enhance the School's reputation. Moreover the building was going from bad to worse: "The schoolhouse is falling into decay and in consequence of this state of affairs we are obliged to seek for our children in the neighbouring villages that education which we think this Charity ought to afford."

The Commissioners' response was to send the Vicar a comprehensive questionnaire. From it we learn that the Assistant Master, Thomas Wood, who was in sole charge, worked full time and for a further two hours one evening, that the children of parishioners were accepted from six years of age, that there were thirty pupils – all free – and the building was "one old room – much dilapidated." The tone of the Revd Snowdon's reply reveals his frustration with those who had complained and with the workings of the School:

> The School might at once be made a hundred times more useful if liberal and practical men were added to the sub-trusteeship who would aid the work by encouragement without increasing or magnifying the difficulties arising in the working of an entirely free School, lending a hand instead of retarding a faltering step. I doubt whether its duties are performed to the satisfaction of any one connected with it. Sub-trustees have induced a feeling to prevail among the parishioners generally that an endowment of £60 to £50 per annum should enable the Vicar to provide a first rate education for the Parish both for boys and girls without any exertion on the Parishioners' part.

The following year, 1865, the Trustees resigned. The Churchwardens then presented a memorial alleging that the delegation of the schoolmaster's duties was contrary to the Decree of 1711 and complaining that, although the Churchwardens had been among the purchasers of the estates in 1701, they were now unrepresented on the Board of Trustees. It all sounds very unpleasant and acrimonious. To cap it all, there had been some financial mismanagement. Not only had the whole of the original £100 been spent on enclosing and walling the Bewerley estate but a further debt of £120 had been incurred, which was having to be paid off by instalments over several years by deducting them from the rents before they were paid to the Vicar, much to his dismay. It was a sorry state of affairs.

In the meantime an educational survey of endowed and proprietary schools throughout the country, the Taunton Commission, was under way and the resulting report in 1868 confirmed that things in Ilkley were indeed in a bad way. In spite of a nominally impressive curriculum, there seemed to be little education of any sort going on. The Assistant Master was "working under great difficulty" since he simply had to admit every parishioner's child, of whatever age, who might turn up. By this time there were forty five on the roll, though only thirty three in attendance, of whom six were girls, "the peremptory restriction once in force to 'male children' having been dispensed with in practice as the school declined in its character to the level of an ordinary village school." The only fee charged was a penny a week "for stationery, cleaning the school and mending the windows." Standards were spectacularly low. Of the "thirteen boys at the head of the school, there were only three who could write a short sentence from dictation, and two who could do an addition sum. Little beyond reading, writing and arithmetic has been attempted, but nothing else has been effectively taught."

Schoolmaster Thomas Wood and pupils stand outside the old Grammar School building in 1869, shortly before it closed.

Matters were even worse with the younger children: "In the lower part of the school it was impossible to find evidence of any teaching or discipline whatever," this in spite of a reference under "Discipline" to "Occasionally a public caning." There were the predictable comments on the building: "The general aspect of the school is most unpleasing, as the premises are old and in bad repair and very ill adapted for school purposes. The schoolroom is inconveniently situated close to the high road, and there is no playground." The inspectors laid the blame for this situation on the outmoded nature of the endowment: "The arrangement which gives a clergyman the nominal mastership while it brings him no profit, is liable to expose him in the neighbourhood to suspicions which are wholly undeserved. There would be no more difficulty in Ilkley than in other places in obtaining reasonable payments from the parent if the instruction given in the school were worth having. The existence of this endowment has done much to hinder the establishment of a good school, either for the poor, or the trading middle class, both of whom are greatly in need of one." The final, damning assessment was that "it is evident that at present the school serves no useful purpose."

Mr Fitch, who wrote the report, (and who, incidentally, as Sir Joshua Fitch was to be the guest of honour at the Speech Day of 1899) was mistaken in his belief that all Ilkley people would willingly pay for for their children's education. Nothing could have been further from the truth. When the Charity Commissioners proposed a scheme for re-establishing the School with the schoolmaster independent of the vicar and the level being

The old Grammar School as it is today.

The blue plaque outside the old Grammar School building on Skipton Road.

raised by extending the range of subjects taught and imposing fees, there was immediate opposition. Public meetings were held and in October 1868 a majority of the population signed a petition saying such a scheme would be "a perversion of the founders' intentions." It was argued that, if everyone were charged, the children of the poor, and probably a good few more besides, would be excluded from education. This was simply not acceptable and hence the proposal was dropped. Instead, energetic fund-raising through grants and subscriptions began for a National School, with a wider curriculum and superior buildings and equipment. The Ilkley Gazette lent its support, stating in 1871 that "the long felt want of school accommodation in Ilkley has, from the greatly increased population of late become a positive necessity." The money was raised and the new school, built on Leeds Road, opened its doors on 22nd July 1872. Thomas Wood became the Head Master of the Boys' National School and Miss Hannah Hartley was appointed Headmistress of the Girls' School. Mr Wood's sense of relief at his new premises is clear from his first entry in the log book: "The new school was opened this week with 32 boys. What a change from the old one where we were so closely packed." As Ilkley Church of England School it went on to provide elementary education for boys and girls until 1950 and, as All Saints School, continued, first as an Infant and Junior School and then as a First School, to serve the town into the twenty-first century. In the meantime, the old Grammar School had ceased to exist by 1871 and the schoolhouse was sold for £200, suffering the indignity of becoming a cobbler's shop before being rented by the Christian Brethren.

That might well have been the end of the story had it not been for one important fact: the Bewerley estates, purchased with

Reginald Heber's bequest in 1701, were still there and partly owned by the School Trustees. These farms, together with some allotments, provided an annual income of over a hundred pounds and when they were sold in 1874 they realised £6,089 14s. When the amount due to the Church had been deducted and the £200 from the sale of the old building was added, the Trustees were left with the sum of £4,260. Heber's bequest had been made specifically to the School and it was this money which ensured its continuation as a grammar school. Thus, and not for the first time in its history, there was the money for a school but there was no building.

Delays

There was soon to be more money. A field called Whitton Croft, where the Library and Town Hall now stand and where the name is still marked by Whitton Croft Road, had been left by Richard Whitton in 1730 to the poor of Ilkley. Eventually it passed to the Grammar School Estate and was seen as a site for a future school. Similarly, land known as Raw Croft or Nest Egg and left to the town in 1669 by Joseph Watkinson became the property of the School, as did funds from the Cow Close Gate Dole Charity, dating back to 1643. These bequests were important in the eventual funding of the new building but their legacy is preserved in a more immediate way to this day. The coat of arms of the Watkinson family, still to be seen on the brass by the Watkinson pew in Ilkley Parish Church, forms the right half of the school crest, while the left half contains the Whitton arms.

INTERRED
Mʳ IOSEPH WATKINSON OCTOBER THE 5ᵗ 1669
Mʳˢ MARY WATKINSON HIS WIFE MAY THE 14ᵗᵉ 1658
Mʳ HENERY WATKINSON THERE SONN FEBRVARY 4ᵗ 1648
MARY LAWSON DAVGHTER TO Mʳ WILFRID LAWSON AND
MARY HIS WIFE WHO WAS SECOND DAVGHTER TO THE
SAID IOSEPH AND MARY WATKINSON IVLY THE 16ᵗ 1662
WILFRID LAWSON SONNᵉ TO Mʳ WILFRID LAWSON AND
MARY HIS WIFE: IVLY THE 22 1671
1671
EDWARDE LAWSON THERE SONNE AVGVST THE FIRSTE

A transcription of the Watkinson brass in Ilkley Parish Church. The Watkinson arms form the right side of the school crest.

By kind permission of the Churchwardens.

In the meantime Ilkley was changing rapidly. The Ilkley Gazette of 24th February 1870 contrasted the old and the new:

> A few of those old visitors who were formerly annual frequenters to Ilkley in quest of retirement and quietness now sadly grieve o'er the change which has taken place within the last few years. Fain would they see the old thatched dwellings, antiquated shops, ugly roads, circuitous award paths, unlighted streets and hear the crack of the coachman's whip as he startled his mettled steeds. All these, alas! to such are forever gone; and no amount of pining over them will ever bring their return. They have been succeeded by what another class of visitors deem modern social improvements – finer and more comfortable dwellings, handsome shops, improved roads and paths, well lighted streets and railway communication.

The coming of the railway in August 1865 was a key factor in the rapid development of the old village into a modern Victorian town. It not only brought visitors to the new hydros and hotels for the hydrotherapy 'cure' but also established convenient access to Leeds and Bradford and encouraged wealthy men who had businesses in those cities to settle in Ilkley. At the same time there was a surge of land available for building and the Gazette cites this, and in particular the sale of land by Mr Middelton, as the main reason for the rapid growth. Between 1867 and 1870 alone there were five major sales by auction, comprising 145 lots, as well as many other private sales of plots of ground. The population in 1841 was 778; by 1871 it was 2,511 and by 1901 it had risen to 7,455.

In 1871 the Endowed School Commissioners produced a Scheme for a new Ilkley Grammar School, which was approved in 1872. It proposed a building for 60 pupils at a cost of up to £1,000 (a ludicrously low estimate), the appointment of a Head at an annual salary of £60 (plus a fixed amount per pupil) and fees of £4 to £10 per year. Boys – for it was to be a boys-only school – would be admitted at eight and could remain until they were seventeen. An extensive curriculum was envisaged. The link with the Church was to be severed and a Governing Body of ten local worthies was constituted. There was only one problem: there was still no building. Hence the Scheme never came into practical operation except for the appointment of a Governing Body and the vesting of the School Estate in the official Trustee of Charity Lands.

Nevertheless hopes were raised. Denton's 'Ilkley Directory, Guide Book and Almanac' for 1871 proclaimed:

We are glad to inform the Ilkley people that this long-neglected school is likely soon to be remodelled, as the Royal Commissioners have intimated that it is on the early portion of their list. We hope the inhabitants of Ilkley will be on the alert, and at once petition for its being adapted to the requirements of the times, so that the children of Ilkley may receive their fair share of a good education free of charge, or nearly so.

The Revd John Snowdon, Vicar of Ilkley from 1842 until his death in 1878.

The appointment of the new Governing Body was an occasion for squabbles and plain speaking. When Mr Fearon, representing the Commissioners, consulted leading residents over the constitution of the Board, the Revd Snowdon objected, to Mr Middelton, the Lord of the Manor, because he was a Catholic and to Mr Hartley, Chairman of the Local Government Board, because he was "not a gentleman." There were even disputes about who should and should not be a governor, with Dr Mcleod of the Ben Rhydding Hydro objecting to Henry Strachan, Acting Manager of Wells House, on the grounds that "it is surely not a suitable thing to make a spirit dealer over whose counter you can purchase and drink Brandy, Gin or Whisky, a governor of a school for boys." Mr Strachan withdrew, whereupon several governors refused to serve with Dr Mcleod, who in any case did not secure nomination. In spite of all this, the Board of Governors was constituted and met for the first time on 9th June 1872.

They welcomed the new Scheme "and it was unanimously agreed that the first thing to do was to erect a school." However, as the Clerk, Mr Margerison, was quick to point out, "to do this money must be raised . . . Until a school is erected the Scheme is entirely inoperative as there is no building in Ilkley to be rented or purchased fitted for the proposed school." Indeed it was to be over twenty years before the new Ilkley Grammar School was born. There were many reasons for the delay. The sale of the Bewerley land became a protracted affair, with the purchaser, Mr Hanley Hutchinson, offering a lower price and the Charity Commissioners holding out for a higher one. When the sale was finally agreed, a Mr Ingleby decided he had an interest in some of the land and the Governors had to come to an agreement to compensate him. Then there were other lands and properties to be sold, particularly in the Crossbeck and Cowpasture areas, each sale proceeding at a snail's pace and generating phenomenal amounts of paperwork. The £1,000 limit on the cost of a building made realistic progress impossible and the Charity Commissioners were not minded to increase it. Indeed they were a major block on progress, for the Governors could spend no money without their permission. In October 1874 the Governors complained to the Commissioners that they already had a site [Whitton Croft] "which costs nothing but a suitable building cannot possibly be erected for the £1,000. Will the Commissioners allow the Governors to have a plan drawn and an estimate obtained for the erection of a "School" or "School and Master's House", such plans to be submitted to the Commissioners for appeal, and then consent to any increased expenditure?" It came to nothing. By 1875 they were complaining that they had plans prepared "but the estimates amount to about £7,000" and they signalled their intention "to rent a suitable house for a temporary school and thus get some idea as to the accommodation it will be necessary to provide."

Arguments rumbled on over Whitton Croft. This site was strenuously supported by the Revd Snowdon, the most influential of the Governors, perhaps because it was next to his new vicarage in Wells Road and therefore more convenient. Snowdon was a remarkable man. He had been Vicar of Ilkley since 1842 and had enlarged the Parish Church in 1860-61 when, during reconstruction, services were held in the Grammar School. He had been a prime mover in the building of the Ilkley Charity Hospital. He had been responsible for the old Grammar School and was on the Governing Body of the new one. He was heavily involved in the establishment of the National School. He had a finger in most pies and did not surrender easily. The Whitton Croft option was opposed by all the other Governors but it was not until the Revd Snowdon died in 1878 that it was finally dismissed. It took the Governors only eleven days to agree that the site was too small. They pointed out to the Commissioners that the population of the town had risen from 2,511 in 1871 to over 4,000, the number of inhabited houses from 397 to 820 and the total rateable value from £15,234 to £29,035. "The Inhabitants," they continued, "are principally Professional and Business men from Leeds and Bradford. A considerable number of children attend the Grammar School at Bradford daily, a distance of 14 miles, some go to Boarding Schools and others attend Private Schools in Ilkley, of which there are four for boys. I think the Governors may safely calculate from 100 to 150 boys attending a Public School in Ilkley when erected."

At the same time there were misgivings among some in the town about the nature of the school proposed. The old question of the payment of fees raised its head. Many felt that such payments went against the spirit of the founders' intentions which had been to provide a free grammar school and that the need to pay would in effect exclude the 'industrious poor' from the benefits of a grammar school education. Others felt that the income would be insufficient to maintain such an ambitious scheme.

As the Governors had indicated, there was a gap in the market which others were quick to fill. Denton's Ilkley Directory for 1871 carries an advert for The High School, Ilkley (Principal: Mr Ingleton) in Parish Ghyll Road:

> Ilkley High School was opened in 1869 and was established for the purpose of providing a high-class educational training for the sons of business and professional gentlemen residing in Ilkley and its neighbourhood. That a great need existed here for such an institution has been abundantly evidenced by the fact that there are already close upon forty pupils in attendance, and the number is continually increasing.

There was Ilkley College, which also opened in 1869 on Queen's Road (later the Deaconess College), where the Principal was Mr Kaye, and the Wharfedale School on Ben Rhydding Road, run by the Revd Mr Burrows, which prepared pupils for public school and university and boasted tennis courts, a carpenter's shop and a gymnasium (with drill instructor). Then there was Burnside School on Wheatley Road, which offered training "for mercantile and professional life" and prepared for Cambridge and London Universities. Additionally there was an array of dame schools for girls; Shuttleworth's 1867 Guide lists boarding schools kept by Miss Adcock at Bilberry Bank, Miss Ward at Crossbeck House, Mrs Brumfitt at Mount Pleasant and Miss Monckman at Alexandra Terrace, while day schools were run by Miss Whittaker at Wood's Place and Misses Urquhart and Rhodes at Bellevue Terrace.

Amid this burgeoning provision, albeit of variable quality, plans for a new grammar school dragged on. As long as the building budget remained at £1,000, permanent accommodation was impossible. There was a scheme to rent a house, there was a proposal from Mr Middelton "who has offered the land behind the Church yard at a reduced price", there was a thought of buying Ilkley College and there was even a proposal for renting the National School building, as long as the managers could retain its use as a Sunday School, but these and other proposals were considered impractical or too expensive. In 1878 the Commissioners raised the figure to £3,000 but by now even this was inadequate, given the rise in building prices and the rapid growth in population. The extent to which the Governors had relied on the Revd Snowdon's knowledge of the various charities and endowments was revealed when he died and they were left to lament, "Mr Snowdon the late Vicar of Ilkley, who alone understood all these matters, is dead." In desperation they requested "an enquiry to be held on the spot or, if the Commissioners would prefer, a deputation of Gentlemen from Ilkley to wait upon them." By 1879 they were at the end of their tether: "The Governors therefore ask that a gentleman should be sent down to Ilkley to meet the Governors and go thoroughly into the matter. As, unless something be done forthwith, the Governors see no alternative but to resign their Trust, public feeling being unmistakeably apparent against further delay." The 1880 Ilkley Directory joined the complaints: "The Charity Commissioners refuse to allow more than a certain sum – totally inadequate – for the erection of a school and residence to replant the building which for generations has answered to the name of 'The Ilkley Grammar School'." The frustration in the town was palpable.

Mr Fearon, Assistant Commissioner, responded in March 1880 by meeting the Governors. In the meantime the following advert had been placed in the Leeds Mercury, the Bradford Observer and the Yorkshire Post: "Wanted to purchase from 3 to 5 acres of land in Ilkley a suitable site for The Grammar School. Particulars and price to be sent to W. Margerison, Solicitor, Bradford." The Governors were keen that the new school should be near the railway station and close to Ben Rhydding, which was expanding rapidly. Two sites were initially considered and dismissed, Whitton Croft (again) because it was still too small and by now the land was too valuable for a school building, and the Ilkley College building because it had no playground. Eventually six possible sites were identified. These included land between the church and the river (as proposed by Mr Middelton), a site on Bolton Bridge Road, another fronting Skipton Road on the south side by Westville Road and one to the west of Ilkley by Chapel Lane. Additionally there were two possible sites on the Sedbergh lands and it was one of these that commended itself to Mr Fearon. In July 1880 there is the first indication that "the Charity Commissioners appear inclined to sanction the purchase of 5 acres of land in the Cowpastures belonging to the Governors of Sedbergh School." The site was on Cowpasture Road, which had developed from the old path from Ilkley to the Cow Pastures, which were on land next to the moor. The history of this land was outlined in a lecture given in 1873 by John Dobson, an Ilkley boarding-house keeper, who was recalling the village of the 1820s:

The Cowpasture had been a plot of land taken from the moor, in which several persons had special rights in the summer, but which was thrown open to the moor from the beginning of October until Mayday. The extent of the Cowpasture was 70 acres. It then consisted of one large field and was undrained, in consequence of which it was said that the cattle were subject to peculiar diseases of which they not infrequently died. The Cowpasture had originally been enclosed with the consent of the Lord of the Manor and some of the principal freeholders; and the persons who had benefit in it before its enclosure were Mr Middelton, the Trustees of Sedbergh Grammar School, and the poor of Ilkley, represented by the Vicar and Churchwardens. A 'cow gate' was reckoned at about three acres [the number of gates determined the number of beasts that could be grazed], and on a particular day, about the first of May, the representatives of the different persons interested attended the vestry of the Parish Church to let the 'gates'. When they were let for £1 each or under they were said to be cheap, and when at or about 30s they were called dear.

Ilkley from the Cow Pastures - an engraving from 1855.

Mike Dixon.

Mr Fearon reported to the Charity Commissioners that the site "faces Cowpasture Road on the south, and a footpath which will probably soon become a road called Springs Lane on the north." It was proposed that the building should occupy "the southern corner", that "the slope in the middle could be terraced" and that "the lower part could be used as a cricket field." The aspect attracted special mention: "The view from the southern end of this site is magnificent, and the situation is in the best and most flourishing part of the town, conveniently near the railway station, and easily approached from all the upper part of the town and from Ben Rhydding." There was even a suggestion that "the frontage to Cowpasture Lane might with advantage be reserved as sites for small Villas or better class dwellings, for which it is especially suitable." On 28th January 1881, the land, which was owned by the Governors of Sedbergh School and had once belonged to the Chantry of St Nicholas, was purchased for £2,420.

It was then decreed that a new Scheme would be needed before matters could progress. Governors' patience was wearing thin and in November 1881 an exasperated Mr Margerison wrote, "When is it likely that the proposed new Scheme will be ready? If something is not done shortly the present Governors will be compelled to resign." The issue over status was settled by the Endowed Schools Commissioners, who said they had no power to alter this aspect of the 1872 Scheme and that the new school would therefore be a grammar school. Accordingly the Scheme, albeit in a form re-drafted in 1881, was maintained and went forward for approval. There were still objections from many in the town, especially over the questions of fees and boarders. The Ilkley Free Press reported a stormy meeting at the Assembly Room on Weston Road. Dr Dobson believed "the School Board . . has not gone far enough, and the working class ought not to rest until they have got their just rights. The money was left specially for the benefit of the poor of Ilkley and therefore they are the people who ought to derive the benefits." John Wilde agreed: "The question is simply this: the money paid to the school fund, is it or is it not the property of the working population? If it is the property of that class, then the least the Charity Commissioners could do would be to give them not a free school but a good elementary school." The Ilkley Gazette reported a School Board election meeting in December 1881: "Mr Cooke said they would remember that at a meeting held in that place three years since, when Mr F.W. Fison spoke, he referred to the Grammar School and promised that he would use his influence to make the school a real benefit in the town. What had been the result? The Grammar School was in about the same position as it was then – it still hung fire (hear, hear)."

When the Governors met in January 1882 to consider the new Scheme, they had to face a deputation of ratepayers whose spokesman, Mr Ibberson, complained that "to apply the doles for the purpose of educating the children of the upper classes was unfair and would be robbing the poor of their just rights as in the old Grammar School the children were educated at a nominal cost." He even suggested the Chairman should call a public meeting to discuss the issue. On 8th February a petition was sent to the Charity Commissioners. It had been drawn up by the Revd H.B.Ottley, Vicar of St. Margaret's and a member of the Ilkley School Board, and supported by 686 subscribers. It requested the approval of an amended scheme so that "the present generation may be enabled to enjoy the benefits of the endowments." In effect it was urging the immediate use of the income from the endowment for a free school below the educational level of a grammar school. The argument was partly undermined by the existence of the National Schools, which, even though they charged fees until 1891, were already providing elementary education. Moreover the Grammar School Governors, all local men of some standing, were prepared to defend their Scheme, having sold the properties, invested the money and purchased a site. They were not to be deflected and declared that, though they would try to keep fees as low as possible, they would resign if the new school were to be "made little better than an elementary one." The matter was settled once and for all when the proposed Scheme was approved by Her Majesty in Council at Balmoral on 6th November 1883.

The Ilkley Grammar School was to be a day and boarding establishment for up to a hundred boys. There was to be a Governing Body of ten, four Representative Governors to be appointed by the School Board of Ilkley for five years and six Co-optative Governors to be appointed by resolution of the Governors for eight years. The Headmaster was to be a graduate of a United Kingdom university and was to live on the premises. His annual salary would be £150 per year. Capitation was fixed at not less than £2 or more than £5 per boy per year. Boarders were to pay not more than £45 a year. The age of admission was eight and no boy could stay beyond seventeen. It "is open to all boys of good character and sufficient health. Before admission each boy is required to pass an entrance examination." This could be graded according to the age of the boy and adapted by the Governors "but it shall never fall below the following standard, that is to say: Reading; Writing from dictation; Sums in the four simple rules of Arithmetic, with the Multiplication Table; Outlines of the Geography of England." Tuition fees were to be fixed by the

AT THE COURT AT BALMORAL,

The 6th day of November, 1883.

PRESENT,

THE QUEEN'S MOST EXCELLENT MAJESTY

IN COUNCIL.

WHEREAS the Charity Commissioners for England and Wales have, in virtue of the powers conferred upon them by "The Endowed Schools Act, 1869," and Amending Acts, and of every other power enabling them in that behalf, made a Scheme, relating to Ilkley Grammar School, in the West Riding of the County of York:

And whereas all the conditions in regard to the said Scheme, which are required to be fulfilled by the said Acts, have been fulfilled: NOW, THEREFORE, Her Majesty, having taken the said Scheme (copy whereof numbered 762 is herewith annexed) into consideration, is pleased, by and with the advice of Her Privy Council, to declare, and doth hereby declare, Her approval of the same.

C. L. PEEL.

The Scheme that ended all the arguments. Once this was approved in 1883, it was clear that the School would be a fee-paying "Day and Boarders' School for Boys."

762.

SCHEME above referred to.

County—YORKSHIRE, WEST RIDING.
Parish—ILKLEY.
Endowments—ILKLEY GRAMMAR SCHOOL
and others.

CHARITY COMMISSION.

In the Matter of the SCHOOL founded at ILKLEY in the West Riding of the County of York in the year 1607, and of certain other Endowments in the same Parish; and

In the Matter of the Endowed Schools Act, 1869, and Amending Acts.

Scheme for the Administration of the Foundation and Endowments above-mentioned or referred to.

1. The Endowments dealt with by this Scheme are:—

So much of the former Endowment of the above-mentioned School as by virtue of a Scheme made under the Endowed Schools Act, 1869, for the management of that School and of the severance made thereunder of part of such Endowment from that School, remains as Endowment of that School under that Scheme; *Future administration of Foundation.*

The Charity of Richard Whitton at Ilkley above-named, now managed under a scheme made under the Endowed Schools Act, 1869;

The Dole Charity known as the Cow Close Gate Dole at Ilkley aforesaid, and applied for the advancement of education by a Scheme made under the Endowed Schools Act, 1869; and

The Dole Charity founded by Joseph Watkinson at Ilkley aforesaid, and applied for the advancement of education by a scheme made under the Endowed Schools Act, 1869.

These Endowments shall henceforth be one Foundation, and shall be administered under this Scheme, under the name of the Ilkley Grammar School, hereinafter called the Foundation.

Governors and to be not less than £5 and not more than £12 a year. Scholarships, giving exemption from fees, were to be available "limited in number in the proportion of not more than one for every ten boys in the School but never less than three." The following were to be "the subjects of instruction":

>Reading, Writing and Arithmetic;
>Geography and History;
>English Grammar, Composition and Literature;
>Mathematics;
>Latin;
>At least one Modern Foreign European Language;
>Natural Science; Drawing, Drill and Vocal Music;
>Greek at an extra fee of £3 a year.

There was to be yearly examination by an external examiner, who should report in writing to the Governors.

Everything, it would appear, was now in place for matters to progress, but, almost inexplicably, it was 1890 before an advertisement was placed for designs for the new building. The intervening years were spent in the writing of hundreds of letters and the resolution of countless issues, negotiating with the Charity Commissioners, revising the size and cost of the building, selling the remaining lands of the endowment (the last property sale, that of Whitton Croft, was not effected until 1891), arguing with tenants and their solicitors, deciding who should "level, metal, pave, kerb and channel a moiety of Cowpasture Road", paying legal bills, identifying rights of way, and even having to comply in 1885 with the insistence of the Local Government Board that a fifteen inch sewer pipe should be driven directly through the site. Amid a welter of correspondence the Board refused the Governors' request that the pipe be diverted and the matter was finally resolved by a compensation payment of £90. The Governors, continually thwarted by the burden of bureaucracy, again threatened to resign if the delays continued. Shuttleworth's Guide to Ilkley for 1884 caught the prevailing pessimism in its section on the Grammar School: "The Governors propounded a new scheme by which their funds were to be applied in the education of a certain number of Ilkley boys. Although twelve years have elapsed since this action was taken, nothing definite has yet been determined on. A scheme of the Commissioners has recently been approved, but as the Governors may find difficulty in disposing of the property there is no immediate prospect of carrying the scheme into practice." It must have been deeply frustrating for Governors to receive a request such as that from Mr Ramsden of Halifax, who, in 1885, clearly believed the School to be a going concern. George Brumfitt, the newly-appointed Clerk, had to respond, "I am in receipt of your

A statement of the School's financial position on July 1st 1890, "specially prepared in view of projected building."

Ilkley Grammar School.

A Statement of the financial position of the Trust on

July 1. 1890,

specially prepared in view of projected building.

	£	s	d
Fund invested in Consols, on which dividends, at rate of £2–15–0 o/o are remitted quarterly to credit of Governors at Bradford Old Bank, Ilkley	7264	3	1
* Deduct sum understood to be set apart as Endowment	6266	13	9
Balance presumably available for building &c.	1000	9	4
This balance represents the amount of Stock produced by the sales to Major Middleton, as follows:— First sale: Purchase money 738–0–0 Stock 745–9–1 Second „ „ „ 248–0–0 „ 255–0–3 1000.9.4			
Credit Balance at Bradford Old Bank, Ilkley, on July 1. 1890	3280	7	—
This includes the following sums recently passed to credit of Governors, and which in accordance with terms of orders authorising sales should be remitted to Charity Commission for investment. Proceeds of sale to Mr C. B. Knapton 288–10–0 „ „ Major Dobson Bros 1400–0–0 1688.10.0			
Amount actually realised & assumed to be available for building	4280	16	4
Estimate of property unrealised.			
Whitton Croft—Total area comprised 8257 sq. yds. Already sold at 10/- per yard Major Middleton, 1st sale 1476 „ 2nd „ 496 1972 Mr C. B. Knapton 577 2549 „ Balance unsold 5708 „			
Estimating this at 12/6 a yard, price would be	3567	10	—
Interest in "The Bruchen", valued on Nov. 28. 1888 at	805	—	—
Grand Total £	8653	6	4

* On addition to this fund of £6266–13–9 there are three several principal sums, portions of proceeds of various sales, which under orders of Charity Commission have been invested to accumulate for various periods, as follows:—

Principal Sum	To accumulate till	Principal & interest to date
866–18–8	Dec. 2.14. 1929	1390 – 19 – 3
204 – 15 – 10	Nov. 27. 1960	293 – 6 – 5
174 – 19 – 5	Dec 20. 1962	262 – 14 – 6
		£1947 – 0 – 2

post card asking for a prospectus from which I conclude that you are under the impression that there is actually a Grammar School in Ilkley. I am sorry to have to inform you that although the Foundation known as the "Ilkley Grammar School" is established, it at present possesses no school buildings. A site has been procured for the projected school buildings but there is as yet no immediate prospect of their being erected." As late as 1886, in the midst of the sewer-induced delays, there was still talk of opening a temporary school.

At long last, on 15th February 1890, advertisements for a building were placed. Designs were required "for School Buildings to accommodate 100 pupils, combined with a Head Master's Residence, containing accommodation for 20 boarders." The Governors seemed confident they could reach these numbers. The population of Ilkley was currently around 6,000 "of whom a more than ordinarily large proportion are of the class that would avail themselves of the advantages offered by the School." Curiously for a new building, it had to be planned "with a view to extension." Whether or not the Governors were hedging their bets at this stage or were hamstrung by the parsimonious Commissioners, it was to be no more than four years before such extensions were needed. Recreation was not ignored. The buildings were to be "so placed as to permit of the northern portion of the land to be utilised as a playground" and "cloisters to be arranged under the School Buildings as a covered playground." The competition was limited to fourteen selected architects, including those of Ripon and Giggleswick Schools, with prizes of £25, £15, and £10 but, being canny Yorkshiremen, the Governors decreed that these designs were to be their property and that, should one of the winners be employed to erect the building, his prize money would be merged into his commission. The plans were displayed anonymously at the Lecture Hall on The Grove and the design of a Bradford and Ilkley architect, Charles Henry Hargreaves, was eventually accepted. The estimated cost was £6,502 5s. Dean Brothers, a local firm, were appointed as masons and work began on 20th June 1892. Even now the Commissioners continued to cause problems. At each stage of the work an architect's certificate had to be sent to Whitehall and the Commissioners had to release the money before the Clerk could pay the contractors. So frustrated were the Governors that they called on the help of Mr Barron, M.P. for Otley, who was even prepared to raise the matter in the House.

In November 1892 the post of Headmaster was advertised and there were a hundred and sixty eight applications. These were whittled down to a short list of five, who were interviewed on Saturday 15th April at the offices on The Grove of local solicitor

The 1890 advertisement for designs for the new Ilkley Grammar School.

Ilkley Grammar School.

COMPETITIVE DESIGNS FOR SCHOOL BUILDINGS. INSTRUCTIONS TO COMPETITORS.

1. Designs are required for School Buildings to accommodate 100 pupils, combined with a Head Master's Residence, containing accommodation for 20 boarders,—both to be planned with a view to extension—with necessary outbuildings.

2. The site of the proposed buildings is on the north side of Cowpasture Road, Ilkley. At present it contains an area of exactly 5 acres, but it is in contemplation to sell off about an acre in area from the south end, abutting on Cowpasture Road; reserving, however, a sufficient width for the formation of the principal entrance from that road. The buildings would have to be so placed as to permit of the northern portion of the land being utilized as playground.

3. Cloisters to be arranged under the School Buildings as covered playground.

4. An estimate of the probable cost of the buildings must accompany each set of plans, and a further estimate must be given of the probable cost of levelling and preparing a sufficient portion of the site for the purposes of a playground.

5. Competitors are requested to observe the greatest economy in the nature of the design for the proposed buildings.

6. Prizes of £25, £15 and £10, are offered for the three most approved designs. The prize designs are to become the exclusive property of the Governors, to be used by them in any way they may think fit. In case the author of one of them is employed to erect the buildings, his prize money shall merge in the commission payable to him.

7. The author's name is not to be marked on the plans, nor are they to bear any distinguishing motto or mark whatever. The name and address of the author are to be enclosed in a sealed envelope, and the plans will be identified with their authors by means of numbers which will be marked on the envelope and on each plan immediately they are received.

8. Each competitor to furnish block plan to scale of 30 feet to an inch. Plans of each floor, also one section and two elevations, to be one-sixteenth scale.

9. All to be drawn in black and white; no colour to be put on either plans, sections, or elevations. The walls on plans to be blacked. The windows in elevations to be blacked.

10. No perspective drawings are to be submittted, and anyone sending in such drawings will be disqualified.

11. All drawings to be mounted on plain stretchers with white borders.

12. One set of plans only to be submitted by each competitor, no alternative plans being allowed, and any infringement of this regulation will be deemed a disqualification.

13. The competition to be limited to fourteen selected architects.

14. All designs to be received by me not later than April 30th, and to be enclosed in sealed cover endorsed " I. G. S. Designs."

GEORGE BRUMFITT,

Clerk to the Governors.

33, Brook Street, Ilkley,
    February 15th, 1890.

Latimer Darlington, Clerk to the Governors. The Board decided to appoint Frederic Swann, who was Head of the Chemistry and Physics Departments at the Royal Grammar School, Newcastle.

On the afternoon of Tuesday 18th July 1893, G.W.Wallace, representing the Charity Commissioners, visited the site to inspect the work. His description, as it neared completion and only two months before it opened, takes us on a fascinating journey through the building in its original layout. It can still be followed by anyone familiar with it today:

The school buildings at the date of my visit were very nearly completed, and it was expected that they would be quite ready by the 1st of August. They consist of a handsome stone building of two storeys of good design, well lighted by mullioned windows, including a central tower with entrances at the front and back, flanked by two wings. The eastern wing on the ground floor is divided longitudinally into two, one half, facing north, forming one large and lofty assembly-room, in which several classes could be accommodated at the same time, and where it is intended that the whole school should meet for prayers at 9am. It is proposed to curtain off one-third of this room for use as an art class-room. The southern half of the wing is divided into three rooms of equal size, one for the head-master's class of senior boys, which will also serve as his library, and the others for junior classes, each room being constructed to hold 20 boys. The ground floor of the tower forms a large entrance-hall, containing the main staircase to the first floor. The back portion forms a cloakroom. Here is the door through which the boys enter, communicating by a winding stair with the cloisters in the basement, at the bottom of which stair is a lavatory. A small room opening at this point into the hall is destined for a laboratory.

The west wing is on the ground floor divided transversely into two portions, of which that next the tower is divided longitudinally into two by a passage. To the south of this passage is the boarders' dining-room, a large room which will hold more than the 20 boarders, and will admit of boys from a distance dining there; to the north the space for the main staircase and the master's private room. The other half of the wing forms the head-master's residence, containing on the ground floor drawing room, dining room, lavatory, store-room and pantry, and provided with a separate main entrance at the south-west corner; and on the first floor three bedrooms, bathroom &c. This part of the

ILKLEY GRAMMAR SCHOOL,

FOUNDED A.D. 1607.   NEW SCHEME A.D. 1883.

Governors.

CHAIRMAN   -   J. C. NAYLOR, ESQ

VICE-CHAIRMAN   -   E. W. CRAWLEY, ESQ.

G. CARTER, ESQ., M.R.C.S

H. DOBSON, ESQ., M.D

JULIAN GREEN, ESQ.

F. H. HUMPHRIS, ESQ

REV. H. KEMPSON, B.A.

C. MOELLER, ESQ.

T. SCOTT, ESQ., M.D.

E. H. WADE, ESQ., J.P.

Head Master.

FREDERIC SWANN, ESQ., B.A. B.Sc. (LOND)

Late Scholar of King's College, London.

AIDED BY AN EFFICIENT STAFF OF ASSISTANT MASTERS.

Clerk to the Governors.

LATIMER DARLINGTON, ESQ., Solicitor, THE GROVE, ILKLEY.

An early advertisement for the School. It carries the new crest, a combination of the arms of the Whitton and Watkinson families.

building is completely shut off on both floors from the school proper. On the first floor of the rest of the building are two dormitories, one 30 feet by 16½ feet, and the other 38 feet by 16½ feet, well lighted, and provided, as all the building is, with patent ventilators. It had not been decided whether to have open beds or cubicles, nor how many boys were to sleep in each dormitory. Between the two dormitories is a bedroom for an assistant-master, commanding each by a small window. Washing accommodation is provided by a large general lavatory containing two plunge baths, a shower bath and wash-hand basins. At the extreme end of this floor, effectively cut off from the rest of it, is a sick ward, with a bathroom &c. The tower rises some little distance above this floor and contains two small rooms, one above the other.

In the basement, which, owing to a fall in the ground forms the ground floor on the north side, there are a large kitchen and scullery with offices and the usual appliances and a boiler-room for hot-water heating apparatus. The extreme north-east corner is a large workshop opening on the cloisters. The latter are under the assembly-room, are well paved, and will be most useful as a playground in wet weather. Connected with the main building at the back are offices, the intervening space being covered with glass, in which bicycles can be stowed. There is a gravelled terrace on the north side, beyond which is the playground, a grass field of several acres, on a considerable slope, which will require levelling in parts if it is intended to be of real advantage for games.

Governors took a keen interest in the details, even down to the placing of a stone plaque in the middle of the tower. Originally it was to have 'IGS' carved on it. Then it was decided to remove it and put a clock in its place. In the event, neither project could be afforded, and there the plaque remains, clearly visible and blank to this day.

The opening had already been advertised with a flourish: "The New Buildings which are to be opened in September are equipped with every modern adjunct, and provide accommodation for Day-Boys and Boarders. The Education given will be that of a High-class Public School." There could be no doubt that, after two decades of delays, the new Ilkley Grammar School was set on an ambitious path.

The New School

Frederic Swann, first Headmaster of the new school from 1893 to 1904.

It opened its doors on the morning of 20th September 1893, though it was barely ready for business. The buildings were incomplete. They were not fully roofed and had no doors or staircases. Mr Swann, while continuing to live and work in Newcastle, had been involved in planning for several months. Now he was camping out in one of the dormitories since his own house was unfinished and thus the building could not yet accommodate its boarders. On that Wednesday morning there was a modest ceremony in the School Hall, now the Drama Studio, attended by Mr Swann, his Deputy Mr Baines, and two governors, Mr Humphris and the Chairman, Mr Naylor, who explained, "On some future occasion there will be a more popular way of inaugurating our school. The Governors feel that as the premises are not complete, it would be scarcely a right thing to have a public ceremony just yet. I extend a hearty welcome to you." Norman Salmon gives a brief account of the ceremony:

The first known photograph of the Cowpasture Road building. On the card, written to Mr Bontoft, Photographer, Wells Road, Mr Swann asks, *"Will you arrange with me to take 3 photos up here of school and boys."*

43

The gathering was small. Thirty eight boys had assembled in the main hall. There was no stage, only a narrow platform or dais, and normally benches, tables or desks filled the area. Mr Swann began with a prayer. Mr Naylor spoke first, exhorting the boys to take advantage of their opportunities and commending their new Head Master. Mr Humphris followed with an account of past difficulties, present problems and future plans. Mr Swann then spoke briefly as to what he expected from them. The boys then began their work.

A report for J.B. Barron in July 1894, at the end of the first year of the new school. It is clear that Mr Swann, as well as being Headmaster, has taught Geography, Grammar, Composition and Spelling, Literature, Reading and Writing, Arithmetic, Algebra and Euclid, Chemistry and Physiology.

REPORT on the Progress and Conduct of *J.B. Barron*
for the Term ending July 27th 1894.
FORM A.   No. of Boys in FORM 20.

General Subjects.

Divinity	Good AS
History	
Geography	} Fairly good. JS.
Grammar, Composition and Spelling	} Excellently prepared
Literature	~~...........~~ at home. JS.
Reading and Writing	Both improved JS.
Singing	Fair AS.
Sloyd Work	
Drill	Very good

Languages.

Greek	
Latin	
French	} Very Satisfactory AS.
German	Von sehr very sat. P. Bauer.

Mathematics.

Arithmetic	
Algebra	} Much steady satisfactory progress. JS.
Euclid	
Higher Mathematics	
Mechanics	

Science and Art.

Chemistry	Good. JS.
Sound, Light, Heat	
Magnetism and Electricity	
Physiology	Good. JS.
Physiography	
Freehand and Model	Freehand very fair. Model drawing fair WJB
Geometrical Drawing	fair work WJB.

Conduct Very good.
Average place in Form 2nd.
Attendance Regular & Punctual.
E. Swann
NOTE—Next Term begins Sept 18th 1894.   Head Master.

The programme for the first Speech Day.

Ilkley Grammar School.

DISTRIBUTION OF PRIZES for the School Year 1893-4,

— IN THE SCHOOL HALL —

— BY —

FREDK. WM. FISON, ESQ.,

— ON —

WEDNESDAY, NOV. 14th, 1894, 7.30 p.m.

Governors:

REV. H. KEMPSON, B.A., *Chairman.*

C. MOELLER, ESQ., *Vice-Chairman.*

G. CARTER, ESQ., M.R.C.S., M.R.C.P.	F. H. HUMPHRIS, ESQ.
E. W. CRAWLEY, ESQ.	F. B. MUFF, ESQ.
H. DOBSON, ESQ., M.D.	J. C. NAYLOR, ESQ.
JULIAN GREEN, ESQ.	T. SCOTT, ESQ., M.D.

Head Master:

FREDERIC SWANN, ESQ., B.Sc., B.A., late Scholar of King's College, London.

Examiner:

(Appointed by the Governors)

PAUL E. SWINSTEAD, B.A., L.C.P., Stationers' Company's School, London, N.

Staff:

A. BAINES, ESQ., B.A., St. John's College, Cambridge.

H. CLEMENTS, ESQ., B.A., St. Catherine's College, Cambridge.

Herr P. BAUER, of Berlin and Paris Universities.

Messrs. W. J. BOYES and E. DOBSON, Art Masters.

Clerk to Governors:

LATIMER DARLINGTON, ESQ., Solicitor, Ilkley.

It was an unpromising beginning and for the first few months there was much to be done. "How we worked together, boys and masters, to improve the place," Mr Swann would later recall. "We built fences, carried tons of stones to form paths, we dug, sowed, planted. Each tree in the grounds could tell a story of those days." Even the Governors were roped in to help plant a beech hedge and over two hundred shrubs.

With only two young and inexperienced assistants to help him – Mr Baines was 21, Mr Clements 22, both Cambridge graduates but with neither training nor experience in teaching – Mr Swann had to establish the new school's reputation locally and further afield, liaise with administrative and examining bodies, make arrangements for boarders, maximise the income, build up the social and sporting life, arrange speech days and before long plan

an extension – and all with no clerical staff. There was stiff competition from local schools and, particularly once the extension was built, there were very limited funds. It was a daunting task.

By December there were fifty boys. They came from Ilkley, Ben Rhydding, Burley and Otley. Most were fee-paying but a limited number of scholarships exempting boys from paying tuition fees were provided. Fees were fixed at £3 6s 8d per term for boys under 12, £4 for those over 12, with additional charges for optional subjects, Greek (£1) Workshop Instruction (7s) and Practical Chemistry (5s). Boarders over 15 were charged £15, those 12-14 £14 and those under 12 £13. They were organised into three forms, one for each full-time master. The ambitious syllabus comprised Divinity, Latin, French, German, English, History, Algebra, Arithmetic, Science, Drawing, Geography, Music and Drill. On 14th November 1894 the first Speech Day was held. Mr Frederick William Fison, distributed the prizes, based on the first of the annual reports of the external examiner, Mr Swinstead. By the next year numbers had risen and there was an additional master and an extra form.

But Mr Swann knew all was not well. As early as February 1894 he was writing to governors, "I have asked to be allowed to

Mr Swann with his staff and pupils in 1897, just four years after the opening of the Cowpasture Road building.

lay before you in an outspoken manner, certain views I entertain as to the present condition, and future work of the School, of its needs and developments, before it can rank amongst the most efficient schools in the District." In particular he was concerned about the low staff salaries and the consequent inexperience and lack of training of his teachers. Fully qualified staff would cost £465 a year; his cost £276. Already, he complained to his governors, the buildings were inadequate. A play room was needed "in which boarders, in wet and cold weather may romp." There was no living room for the masters. Laboratories and other specialist rooms were required. The School Hall doubled up as the Art Room. Library provision was poor. He spoke feelingly of his own living conditions next to the school kitchen: "No one but an inmate in the Headmaster's house can realise the noise, the bustle, the constant rattle of plates, dishes etc. outside his dining room and adjacent to his drawing room. Nor is the all-pervading smell of cooking and washing up dishes an additional charm to the Headmaster's life." Science accommodation and equipment were particular issues; the examiner had even reported that candidates were entered for exams in Physiology when the School did not possess a skeleton.

Governors went back, cap in hand, to the Charity Commissioners to ask for £4,000, the estimated cost of the necessary extensions. The Commissioners agreed to release £2,500 of endowment capital, the estimate was revised down to this figure and the County Council said they would fund half the furniture. So building work began in the summer of 1897 on what became known as the 'northern extension' – in effect those parts of the old building beyond the Entrance Hall. The architect was again Mr Hargreaves and the builders Dean Brothers but matters did not go entirely smoothly. Governors "were not satisfied with the progress of the works" and threatened "that unless the Buildings are ready by the time fixed in the Contracts they will most certainly enforce the penalty clause." Then there was a suggestion of chicanery and a special meeting had to be called "to consider the allegations of certain dealings between one of the Contractors and the Clerk of Works. It was considered the case would be sufficiently met by censuring both." Even when the building was finished, Governors were dissatisfied with some of the work and "sought an assurance from Mr Hargreaves that all the defects be attended to and remedied, and more particularly as to the defective joints and pressed-bricks." Nevertheless Mr Swann was granted many of the rooms for which he had campaigned so vigorously. They included an Art Room, a Workshop, Chemical and Physical Laboratories, two small Music Rooms, an extra classroom and a gymnasium complete with racks for 100 Indian clubs, 100 dumb bells, 50 bar bells and 50 sword sticks. In all, it was a significant addition and it was to be the last major building programme until the 1960s. It was opened on 8th December 1898 by Sir Swire Smith, who was presented with a silver key to mark the occasion. The sanatorium Mr Swann had requested could not be afforded but it was eventually built in 1912 and is now the Caretaker's house.

Ilkley Grammar School had become the largest in the area but it still needed to raise its profile. In a splendid piece of snobbery the Times was asked to insert its notices under the heading 'Public Schools' rather than 'Educational'. There was even an unsuccessful attempt to change its name to 'The Royal Grammar School of Ilkley'. Sporting prowess enhanced prestige, so rugby and hockey fixtures were arranged with schools such as Giggleswick and Woodhouse Grove. Cricket matches were organised with other schools, and against local teams such as Ilkley Tradesmen and Craiglands 'Gentlemen', who, intriguingly, boasted two ladies. Attempts were made to improve swimming facilities. When in 1901 the only swimming bath in the town closed, Mr Swann tried to take it over but the local laundry refused to allow water to be passed through its meter, even though a premium in addition to the cost of the water was offered. So he arranged for the pool to be filled, via the town's fire hose, from the mains, until a leakage rate of 1,000 gallons a day made the whole venture impossible.

There were other problems. A particular handicap was the lack of playing fields. It was met in part by levelling the area at the bottom of the site but, more substantially, by the eventual purchase in 1904 of a field in Ben Rhydding at a cost of £1,000. This was partly offset by the sale of land adjacent to Springs Lane for the Coronation Hospital. Then there was a long-running dispute with the Sedbergh Governors and the Urban District Council over payment for the construction of the new road at Springs Lane. Of course as a boarding school it was also vulnerable to epidemics; in March 1899 the Headmaster reported on "the visitation of Influenza in the School, and that he had received notices from a large number of parents as to the withdrawal of their boys, and in consequence he would have to reduce the staff after midsummer unless a sufficient number of new boys be entered."

This touched on the main problem Mr Swann had to grapple with, finance. The new buildings had reduced the capital and hence the endowment now scarcely met the overheads. To make matters worse, the terms of the endowment prevented him from increasing fees to meet losses. In any case raising the fees would simply have meant losing more boys to other schools – and competition was fierce, with three other schools in Ilkley and

Governors had every reason to be unhappy with the quality of much of the building work in the new extension.

ILKLEY GRAMMAR SCHOOL.

CRITIQUE OF BUILDING.

HENRY DOBSON, JULY 14, 1898.

BASEMENT.

1 LAUNDRY. Walls bad. Up to one inch between ends of bricks, and joints up to three quarters of an inch thick.

2 HEATING CELLARS. Walls are built crooked, and 'bond' is bad in places. North face of old wall is not pointed in Cement—as specified.

3 NORTH ELEVATION. A Crack is seen about the middle of each of the side window-cills, and these cracks can be followed down outer face of wall several yards. How much they will yet extend is quite unknown.

4 OUTER ENTRANCE. 'Boasted' work not built straight. Wall not properly tied into old building.

5 FLAGS at top of stairs. Not 'joggle joints'—and bad square joints. The flags are built into the wall—and could not easily be removed.

6 WALLS IN CORRIDOR. Very badly built—bed of brick 2½ inches out of level in a length of about 18 feet on East side. West side over 2 inches out of straight face in a length of about 22 feet. Also out of perpendicular 1 to 2 inches. Bond defective.

7 STEPS chipped and damaged. Not protected.

8 JOINER'S SHOP. Walls bad and not straight. Joints and faces all bad. 'Throughs' in outer wall notched down (one broken). Other 'throughs' at windows, and for beams, slobbered with lime up to 2 inches thick. 'Throughs' out of course. Brick work at door and windows out of straight, and same with 'boasted' work.

9 GYMNASIUM. All walls bad; not straight in any direction. Joints half to ¾ inch thick. Corners all bad, especially South East,—out of course. East wall courses not level. Face of wall sometimes an inch out of true in 4 to 6 feet. In North wall, throws are out of course, and brickwork patched. In West wall, courses vary up window sides. Consider brick work all bad. Wood Beam no. 2 from West, green and sappy.

10 WEST CLASS ROOM. Pressed brick work all bad.

11 DARK ROOM. Same.

GROUND FLOOR.

12 BOARDERS' PLAY ROOM. Walls not straight. Bad joints. Through stones carrying Iron Girders not in course. *Leaning* brick pillar, carrying beam. Green wood beam, no. 1 from South.

13 ART ROOM. Walls not straight. No bond to brickwork near door. No stone throughs to brick arches (5 in each are specified). This seems important, because pressure is now separate on inner brick arch—and on outer stone arch.

14 GOVERNORS' ROOM. Boasted work at windows out of straight.

UPPER FLOOR.

15 ROOM LOOKING EAST. In this room varying work is shown—before the advent of the Clerk of Works, and since. In S. W. corner is seen that 12 courses of bricks built under the eye of the Clerk of Works occupy the space of 11 courses which were walled before any Clerk of Works.

GENERAL.

16 DOORS & WINDOWS. All 'boasted' work bad—so that wood frames cannot be put in.

17 It would appear that the Architect has not been sufficiently explicit in specification as to the quality of the Pressed Brick work, *which is now supposed to be finished.*

18 The Builder said to the Committee—"Gable and top bit has cost more than all else of building put together."

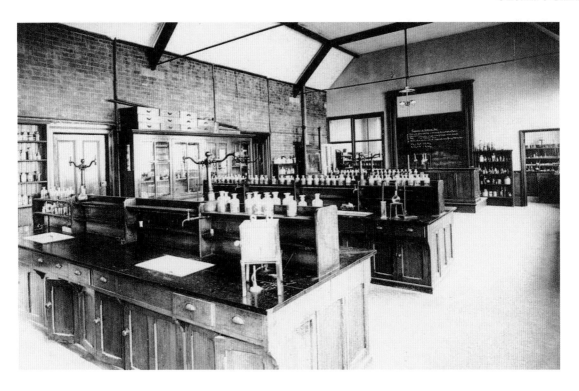

The extensions of 1898 provided specialist accommodation lacking in the original building and necessary if the School was to compete with its rivals. Seen here are the Chemical Laboratory and the Workshop.

A new Gymnasium and Art Room were also provided.

From 1893 until the early 1930s the School took boarders. Here, in the early years of the twentieth century, is a dormitory. The dormitories were on the top floor where there are now laboratories.

relatively cheap train fares to those in Skipton, Shipley, Leeds and Bradford, "each of which offer special attractions and, being within easy reach of Ilkley, draw a considerable number of boys resident in this locality." He tried unsuccessfully to increase boarding fees from £45 to £65 a year. He solicited the rail company to improve the train service but to no avail. He did manage to provide free rail passes "for the railway fares are the chief obstacle in the way of Otley people sending their children here." Eventually he concluded that, since Ilkley could not provide day pupils in sufficient numbers, the Grammar School's future seemed to lie primarily as a boarding establishment on account of "the healthy and picturesque situation of Ilkley which draws from the towns a number of boarders and almost from the beginning of its new career this School has had its full complement of boarders, viz: 20." Yet even this was scarcely enough to make ends meet for, as he complained to the Governors, "with the present fees, and being unable to take more than twenty boarders, the boarding arrangements are practically a source of loss rather than profit."

There was an attempt to take more boarders. Mr Wheater, Head of the Modern School in Thirsk, wrote to Mr. Swann in January 1895, "I am going to have a rather bad term here, as four of my boarders have left and as yet I know of no new certainties for next term. You will understand why I am anxious to leave Thirsk as soon as possible. My expenses are very heavy and I should hardly like to run the school at a big loss for six months." A few days later the situation is even worse: "I am seriously thinking of closing my school unless I receive some applications before Monday. The prospects of private school masters in general and of myself in particular are not bright and I feel inclined to turn my hand to something else." He approached Mr Swann with a plan to open a hostel for boarders in Ilkley. Mr Swann gained permission from the Governors and Mr Wheater, bringing some of his own boys across from Thirsk, took over a house on Wheatley Road. It went well at first and by 1896 it was full but then there was a dispute over how he managed the hostel and the experiment came to an end when he left in 1898.

There is ample evidence of tight finances. In 1898 Mr Swann decided he could no longer afford to rent a pitch from Ilkley Cricket Club: "As we are restricted to Wednesday afternoons for our matches and get only a little over an hour's practice in an evening before you require the field, we have come to the conclusion that we can no longer afford to pay so great a price for so small privileges." In the same year the Governors told him that "as a result of the great increase in expenditure in connection with our Building Extension" he must lose the services of a teacher, Mr. Jefferson, to whom a clearly unhappy Mr Swann had to write, "I regret to say that they inform me that I must rescind the engagement I have with you." When the West Riding decided to increase its grant, provided the School accepted more free places, the Governors received news of the increase "with satisfaction" but were less happy with the strings attached and replied, "Hitherto you have not filled the whole of the free places at your disposal, and the Board trusts that, while nominally accepting the

The Boarders' Dining Hall in the early 1900s. It was "a large room which will hold more than twenty boarders, and will admit boys from a distance dining there." It is now the main school office.

The Boarders' Play Room and Library around 1900.

conditions attached to the grant, you may not find it necessary to fill the whole of the free places." Soon he was going cap in hand to the West Riding to ask for more money to continue employing Mr Dobson, the Art teacher, and in so doing laid before the Council the state of the finances:

> We have an excellent Art Master, capital Art equipment and admirable Art Rooms but recently our endowment has been much reduced by our Expenditure on New Buildings and we now receive therefrom about £150 per annum. Our only other source of income [apart from the County's £100 grant] is from the fees of the pupils – about 80 boys – ten per cent of whom are by our Scheme admitted as Free Scholars. As our rates and taxes amount to £90 per annum and Caretaker's wages, coals and gas amount to about £150, it will be seen that our position financially is of the straitest.

The belt-tightening came even closer to home when, "in consequence of the silence of the Governors" no provision was made in a new draft Scheme for a contribution to the Headmaster's pension from the income of the Foundation. Mr Swann was at pains to clarify the situation:

> It is not always well to take the silence of a Board of Governors as an expression of opinion and in the present case my Board felt that whatever Scheme might come into force in respect of Pensions, the present income of the

School was not sufficiently large to admit of any payments being made towards a Pension Fund for the Headmaster. The paper was therefore simply laid on the table and nothing resolved or even discussed.

Amid such economies, the School was examined each year from 1894 until 1906, partly by written papers and partly by 'viva voce', by an outsider appointed by the governors and reporting to them. Though slight documents in terms of modern reports, they give a snapshot of the curriculum and general levels of achievement. In the early years the examiner, at a fee of £15, was Paul E Swinstead BA, LCP, Second Master at the Grammar School of the Worshipful Company of Stationers, Hornsey. In 1895 he acknowledges early problems but is able to report that "the difficulties attendant on the opening of the School are fast disappearing and I find better order, better arrangement and better work all round." By this time the School was divided into four forms, A to D, by age, soon replaced by the more familiar Third to Sixth Forms. This caused its own problems for, as the 1896 report points out, "The division into four forms does not represent all the sub-divisions, for in each form there are at least two sections." Forms A and B, the oldest boys, were examined in 1895 in Divinity, English, Latin, French, German, Arithmetic, Algebra, Euclid, History, Geography, Drawing and Writing and, although there were slight variations, this remained, for some years, the staple curriculum. There is a general sense of improving standards and comments are mostly positive. Sometimes there is terse

"Big School" in the early years of the twentieth century. It served as the School Hall from 1893 until 1964. It is now the Drama Studio.

criticism: "Four papers in Arithmetic obtained high marks. The rest were neither neatly nor accurately done"(1903); "As usual there was a remnant which hardly made any response to teaching that had produced good results on the rest" (1901). More typical is: "During the oral Examination I found the boys well behaved and the discipline good. The answers were prompt and, on the whole, intelligent" (1902), while it is reassuring to learn that "the class I heard sing were being trained to be true in tone and tune and to sing sweetly" (1898).

In the Spring Term of 1900 the first edition of the school magazine, the Olicanian, burst onto the scene with a bellowing "Oyez! Oyez! Oyez!" and lots of topical references to the Boer War. Vol. 1 No. 1 was a slim production that included an erudite feature on 'Our Coat of Arms and How We Got It' (Part 1), an account of a mock trial in which the prisoner escaped, news that the school hens had laid a record 22 eggs and an undertaking "that the Olicanian will be posted to any part of the British dominions for a whole year for the sum of one shilling payable in advance." The 'School Notes' reported breathlessly:

The keenest excitement was caused by a telegram in the Post Office on March 1st, which stated that Ladysmith had been relieved the night before. Petitions were at once sent up to the Head Master for a holiday. After dinner we ascertained that the news was official. Three masters and two boys at once rushed up to the tower and hoisted the flag amidst deafening cheers from the rest of the boys in the playground. Needless to say, the holiday was given.

More celebrations soon followed in the next issue:

If the excitement over the relief of Ladysmith was great, that over the relief of Mafeking was even greater. The glorious news arrived at about ten o'clock on Friday night, May 18th. Instantly Ilkley was awakened by the sound of church bells, shots, rockets and a big crowd very soon gathered in the streets. The Town Band played National tunes till after midnight.

(An interesting footnote is that Mr Whiteley, the Mayor of Mafeking during the siege, not only settled in Ilkley but was a governor during the 1920s.)

The feature on the Coat of Arms, designed by Mr Swann, which ran across the first two issues, showed that much research had gone into finding out whether the Watkinson and Whitton families possessed a 'coat':

The first edition of the Olicanian - Spring Term 1900.

The Olicanian

THE
MAGAZINE
OF

THE ILKLEY
GRAMMAR
SCHOOL.

Vol. I. No. 1.   SPRING TERM, 1900.

Editorial.

Oyez! Oyez!! Oyez!!!

Here we are, and how do you like us, as the lyddite shell said when he dropped into the Boer trenches.

Sorry to inconvenience you, good friends, *Times*, *Punch*, and *Nineteenth Century*, but kindly sit a little closer, or two of you get on to one chair if you like, and make room for your uncle, *The Olicanian*.

Apologise? Not a bit of it. Did "Bobs" apologise when he asked Cronje to make room for him? Did Shakespeare apologise when he walked to the top of English literature?

We all know, don't we, that Ilkley is one of the prettiest spots in the world, and that its school is certainly the best Grammar School in Yorkshire, if not in England, and it is in the endeavour to complete the education of the B. P. (British public—not B-d-n P-w-ll) in this respect, that the *Olicanian* makes its bow to the world.

Come, then, you village Hampdens, you mute inglorious Miltons, who are only waiting for an opportunity of shining

The case of J. Watkinson was soon solved, for in the Ilkley Parish Church you may find a brass let into the west wall, near the old squire's pew, on which are the very arms of this Joseph Watkinson. That portion of our shield on the right-hand side of the medial line is the 'coat' of Joseph Watkinson. You will notice that it is divided into four quarters, indicating that he is linked with another family, whose arms appear in two of the quarters. This portion containing an inverted V, known in heraldry as a 'chevron,' was found to be the 'coat' of the Lawsons of Cumberland, of which family Sir Wilfred Lawson is the living representative, and the crest which will be seen over the Watkinson brass is Sir Wilfred Lawson's own crest.

The Whitton side of things caused more trouble:

It was ultimately found that the family of Whitton in this neighbourhood had the right to 'wear' the coat herein represented. Its description, in the quaint language of heraldry, informs you that "on a field, sable, a water-budget, argent, three roundels in chief, or," which being interpreted means that the curious device something like a M, lies on a black ground, and at the top of the shield are three golden spots. The 'water budget' has quite a history in itself. It is now a purely conventional device, but formerly was a rough drawing of two leathern water skins, one on each side of a yoke-saddle. In crusading days this would be a common sight, and the device would indicate in strict heraldry that the wearer of such a coat, or his ancestors, had taken part in the crusades. The crest of the Whitton family was found to be an owl "ducally gorged," which has no reference whatever to its gastronomic performances, but merely indicates that it has a ducal coronet around its throat.

Finally a motto was required:

So wits were set to work to contrive a fitting legend appropriate to the School. Finally the words from the Latin Vulgate, slightly altered, were adopted. You will find them translated from the original in the last verse of the 2nd Chapter of St. Luke, and as they stand in our coat of arms, "Sapientia Et Statura Proficiamus" they mean "May we grow in wisdom and stature."

Soon there was an Old Boys' Association with Mr Swann as President and the first Annual Dinner, attended by thirty two Old

Olicanians was held at the Lister's Arms on 30th November 1901. The Old Olicanian magazine joined the Olicanian and together they gave a detailed account of the School at work and play as well as reaction to national events and local and international news from Old Boys. Mr Cramphorn, the Science master and Mr Biggs, who taught English and French, were the first editors of the Olicanian and almost sixty years later Mr Cramphorn wrote some memories of those distant days:

The cover of the Attendance Book for the Old Boys' Association Annual Dinner.

The Headmaster was the well loved Frederic Swann, an ideal presiding officer, enthusiastic, learned and popular, who, with his wife, established in the school its solid basis of virtue, learning and manners. Boys used to assemble in the games field at the back of the school buildings, and where I believe a donkey, much appreciated by the Headmaster's children during the holiday, roamed at leisure.

A few minutes before 9am the boys lined up in the forecourt and marched into assembly in the big hall, where Mr Swann conducted prayers from the platform. This platform was a punishment for rowdyism in the dormitory at night; offenders were ordered to dress and spend an hour or so thereon, till their exuberance had cooled down.

Many of Mr Swann's letters survive, a unique record of school life over a hundred years ago. As befitted a man soon to be a barrister, he had a precise, direct written style, well illustrated in the curious affair of the bat and the cap. The following letter is addressed to Mr. Lancaster Junior who must have been duly chastened to receive it one morning in June 1898:

When you called on me early in May in reference to a bat and a cap which we found you had removed from these premises, I accepted your statement that you had merely removed them to punish certain of our boys whom you considered to be behaving badly. Whatever the conduct of the boys, you had no right to remove any of their property and I accepted your word that you would repay the value of the goods removed – namely 5/- for the bat and 1/6d for the cap. A few days afterwards the bat was found lying in the School field in a prominent position. Who returned it I do not seek to know. The cap has not been returned nor have you (although I have allowed ample time for re-payment or restoration) paid up the 1/6d which you undertook to pay as the value of the cap. Now therefore take notice that unless this amount be paid, or unless a new Grammar School cap such as Mr. Wright, draper of The Grove, supplies to our boys, be sent in place of the cap you removed, I shall place the matter in the hands of the police to prosecute you for robbery with violence.

Lest it be thought that vandalism and rudeness are modern traits, his letter of October 1898 to a fellow Head (school unknown) should set the record straight:

I am sorry to write in complaint to you of the conduct of certain members of the Football Team who came over here to play our boys yesterday afternoon. We are not fortunate enough to possess a pavilion on our field and the team were shown into a classroom to undress and dress. The conduct of which I must complain is that certain boys have wilfully damaged School property, in a most wanton manner. The desks, which are new pitch-pine varnished, have been deeply scored on their upper surfaces by boot nail marks – evidently the boys have been standing on them, inkpots have been emptied of their contents into the desks, and in the School Hall, quite out of the path to and from the classroom, a life-sized cast of 'The Gladiator' has had the usual 'fig-leaf' broken off. I should know the youth who committed this offence. I happened to enter the Hall as he was just removing his walking stick from the hand of the figure. I did not notice the damage at the moment, as the youth was smoking, and my attention was drawn to this latter fact and I appealed to him to desist. He replied somewhat insolently. After considering the matter quietly I feel that I must ask the Captain of the Team for a written apology for these offences against decency and good behaviour, or failing that I must cancel the return match. Believe me that it is a most unpleasant duty for me to write to you as above but I think you would be the first to deplore the conduct of the Team – or some of its members – and to wish them to make an apology.

Then there is the intriguing affair of the "disgraceful" postcard, evidently sent by a boarder to his brother in Halifax, and for which the father blames the School. Mr Swann, in one of his last letters as Headmaster, written in July 1904, ventures to disagree:

I have yours of the 19th containing the disgraceful postcard which David wrote to his brother. I should be well within what is usual if I expelled him for such a business but I cannot see any way to blacken the whole of his future career in the way in which an expulsion from a Public School does cast a shadow over a boy's life. I have administered a punishment which he will not forget to his last day, but I feel there is some deep-seated evil which I cannot reach, nor cure, which influences at home, of which I am ignorant, are the cause; were it not so no boy would have dared to write to a brother in such a manner or to speak thus of his mother. It is useless to throw the blame at the school. It would need a private detective to follow a boy and see that he does not buy or write a postcard home. He does not learn these things at school, and you must seek in Halifax for the evil influences which are working on the boy. If his own story is believable, he should be sent quite away from home in the holidays; and the sooner he can be started amongst new and good influences the better for him as certain things in Halifax are leading him to ruin.

Nor was he on the best of terms with the Ilkley Gazette, especially when it kept omitting his adverts:

In your issue last night I do not find the advertisement of our Prize Distribution on the 28th inst. When I gave you the order some ten days ago I asked specially for its insertion in the issues of last Friday and yesterday, and I further requested that it should not be forgotten. On two previous occasions in former years you have done exactly the same thing and omitted our specific advertisement in the last issue of the paper before the event. As I wrote very forcibly when ordering this advertisement and asked that it should not be forgotten as I had in mind the two previous lapses, and as you omit all reference to the Prize Distribution in your list of forthcoming events, I can only conclude that this is done <u>deliberately and to give annoyance</u>. I shall decline to pay for the advert of last week as it is no good to us to half perform your contract, and I shall submit the whole question of advertising in the Gazette to my Board of Governors.

The regular meetings of the Governors were minuted in a weighty tome in impeccable copperplate handwriting. Besides the important matters, there are minor entries that catch the eye. In 1898, in an early example of co-education, the Head reported that "the Principals of one of the Ladies' Schools in Ilkley would like to be allowed to send a few of their older pupils to attend the lessons in Chemistry and that a fee would be paid for their attendance." In 1900 fame might have come to Ilkley, for it was reported that "the School had sent up to the Educational Exhibition in Leeds exhibits of work done in design and views of the School premises, and that the West Riding County Council had forwarded same to London to be adjudicated upon as to the exhibits to be sent to the Paris Exhibition." In 1904 Governors had to act to scotch rumours that the School's scholarships were closed to some boys; they resolved "to write to the Ilkley Gazette, the Ilkley Free Press, the Yorkshire Post, the Leeds Mercury and the Yorkshire Observer in order to correct certain views expressed in some of these papers that the free scholarships are not obtainable by the class for whom they were intended." There are regular records of boys winning scholarships. Of three reported in February 1900, two, Henry Eagle and George Dean were later to be Chairman of Governors. Another name to occur regularly down the years is that of John William Dixon. He was appointed Clerk to the Governors in October 1903 and continued to serve in that role until well into the 1930s.

These years also saw the development of local government. In 1888 the Local Government Act created sixty county councils, among them the West Riding, and in 1894 the Local Councils Act created the Ilkley Urban District Council. In 1899 the Board of Education was established, taking over the Charity Commission's responsibilities for education. The School enjoyed the support of the West Riding from the outset, for it contributed pupils through its free places scheme and income in the form of an annual grant. Thus in 1901 when numbers dropped to 69, the County Council paid £125 and reserved 12 places, though it rarely filled its allocation. Under the terms of the 1902 Balfour Education Act, the West Riding County Council became responsible for all levels of education and was to remain so until local government was reformed over seventy years later. It supported the School by grants on condition that it admitted a certain number of county scholarship winners via the County Minor examinations. County representatives formed a large proportion of the governors and their opinions tended to reflect national and county priorities. On the other hand, the co-optative governors continued to see themselves as the backbone of the Governing Body, the trustees of the Grammar School foundation and tradition.

In the meantime Mr Swann felt he was being ground down by the demands of the job. When, in October 1900, he wrote to the Governors expressing concern at a proposed reduction in Mr Dixon's hours, his letter became a cri de coeur. In four closely-written pages he lists the many tasks, some major, others necessary but trivial, which he is bound to carry out unaided. He concludes:

> I cannot play fast and loose with this clerical work. It has to be done and it has grown to be more than I can cope with single-handed. I fear that you would soon weary of coming here night after night, week in week out and stewing in my office for 3 hours per night. Yet that is what has to be done. I have to do it but it is at the sacrifice practically of all social and family life and I can only rarely steal an evening for recreation . . . If I coolly shelve him [Dixon] in favour of your proposal I may simply 'do for' myself. He might not choose to come back and I should be crushed by the sheer

The Rugby 1st XV - 1903. Fourth from the left in the back row is James Croysdale .

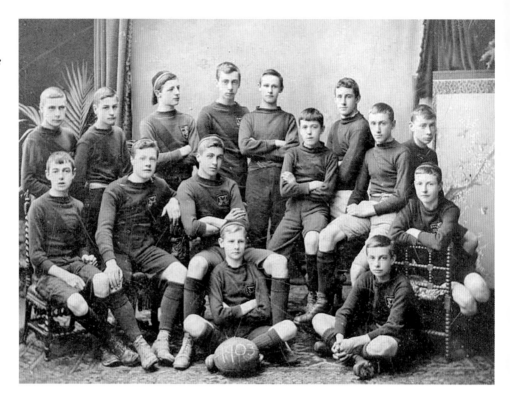

Ilkley Grammar School

DISTRIBUTION of PRIZES

Principal Speaker

The Lord Mayor of Leeds

ALDERMAN SIR JAMES CROYSDALE

on

Friday, 4th November, 1955

at 7 p.m.

in the

KING'S HALL, ILKLEY

Chairman: Mr. Harry Eagle

The programme for the 1955 Speech Day — by which time James Croysdale had made his way in the world.

overweight of work . . . The sooner we have a meeting of the Board and lay this letter before them and thrash the whole matter out, the better, for I cannot go on much longer with things as they are.

There was also a major worry over numbers, which were beginning to fall. The original building, without the extension, had been designed for 100 pupils. All had gone well for a while. From the 50 boys in 1893, numbers had risen to 102 by 1898 but there followed a steady decline, until by 1902 there were only 64 and Governors were beginning to express concern. In the same year there came the first general inspection. The report was less than positive:

A general view of the school field at a Sports Day in the early years of the twentieth century. Middleton Woods are in the distance while, on the field, boaters are being worn.

It is to be regretted that the numbers of the School have decreased of late years. Although the recent depression in trade is regarded as one cause of this, it appears possible that it may also be due in part to the School failing to meet the exact requirements of the boys who use it. The fees are high. The poorer classes find it cheaper to send their sons to the Higher Grade School in Leeds while, on the other hand, parents who desire a first grade education for their boys are inclined to send them to the Grammar School at Bradford. An improvement in the teaching and the qualifications of the assistant masters would bring an increase in numbers.

At a meeting with Governors the inspectors made several suggestions. They proposed "that a Preparatory School might be held

to which children under the age of 8 years and of both sexes might be admitted." They were concerned about the lack of a level playing field and "when they heard of the field which had been offered, and the price asked for it, said it seemed an opportunity not to be lost." They even thought that the proposed new grammar school at Otley might be made all-girls "so as not to compete with the Ilkley Grammar School." One of the inspectors "doubted whether the Governors should reduce the hours for the teaching of languages for mere science." All agreed that the Head did too much teaching. Then, having delivered themselves of their wisdom "the Inspectors and Governors adjourned to the School Hall for evening prayers which were read by the Revd J. Smith."

It was clear all was not well, that some of the early momentum had been lost and that there was unease between Headmaster and Governors. At a meeting on 8th April 1902 "the Chairman referred to his letter to Governors relating to the present state of the School, and the low number of Scholars attending, and as to the best means to make the School better known. He thought the Staff should be improved and the School brought more prominently before the public." Governors were also unhappy at the Headmaster's habit of employing part-time staff without consulting them and decided they would fix the number of assistant masters at the beginning of the school year. Mr Swann seems to have had alternative career plans, for in 1904 he was called to the Bar and resigned his Headship. At the same time all staff contracts were terminated and he was left to hope "that his successor would reappoint them, particularly Mr Dobson."

It was a sad ending to Mr Swann's headship, which had begun with such high hopes in 1893. Almost single-handed he had established the School, managed it on a day-to-day basis, taught much of the curriculum, prioritised and overseen the extensions and presided over an increasingly parlous financial plight. He had worked tirelessly and continued to be held in high esteem by his former pupils. He occupies a special place in the School's history as the first Head in the new building. He remained a frequent visitor, especially to Old Boys' Dinners, where the 'Swann Boys' were always conscious of their unique status. Nevertheless one senses a weariness and frustration towards the end, a feeling that he had given all he could and that it was time for a new, energetic input. It was not to be long in arriving.

J.H.Eddison, a pupil between 1901 and 1904, went on to become a Rugby International, playing for England in 1912.

Edwardian Heyday

Corbett Wadsley Atkinson, Headmaster from 1904 to 1915.

The new Head, Corbett Wadsley Atkinson, Head of Normanton Grammar School, was appointed from 211 applicants in July 1904. The terms of his employment were set out and signed: "A yearly stipend of One Hundred and Fifty Pounds, a yearly capitation fee of Three Pounds for each boy in the School, the house to be free to me of rent, rates and taxes; also the Governors to pay one guinea per week towards the cost of a man as caretaker and gardener etc. as heretofore but the cost of fuel and gas consumed in respect of the house and boarders' and assistants' accommodation shall be borne by myself alone." The Governors were taking no chances; in a further declaration he had to undertake that he would "to the best of my ability discharge the duties of Head Master of the Ilkley Grammar School during my tenure of the office, and that if I am removed therefrom I will thereupon acquiesce in such removal and relinquish all claim to the mastership and its future emoluments, and deliver up to the Governors, or as they direct, possession of all the property of the School then in my possession or occupation."

He lost no time in letting the Governors know his proposals for the School, his preface uncannily prefiguring National Curriculum pronouncements almost a century later:

Fourteen years' experience, a desire to provide a good general education on modern lines for every pupil, and the Board of Education Regulations for Secondary Schools compel me to make certain alterations to the Time Table. It will be seen in the Regulations that a minimum time must be allotted to various branches of the curriculum thus preventing undue specialisation before the age of 16 and guarding against any branch occupying too great a prominence to the detriment of others.

German was to be dropped. Too much time was spent on Art. There was too little Science and insufficient Manual Instruction apparatus. He wasn't keen on the Head acting as a glorified bookseller and he thought the collection of fees "somewhat irregular and complicated." Other changes followed swiftly. He was concerned that numbers had fallen and recognised that he was in competition with private schools, many of which accepted pupils at an early age. He therefore established in 1905 a Preparatory Department, "a form to which small boys, who have reached years of discretion, but are below the age of eight, are admitted." It was housed in the Governors' Room, which became the Library, and was overseen by a newly-appointed Preparatory Mistress. He was also dissatisfied with the ad hoc examination conducted by an individual examiner and saw an opportunity not only to standardise assessment but to raise the profile of the School locally. Hence he proposed that it should be carried out by "some recognised authority, such as the University of Oxford," and that the School "should become a Local Centre for a combined School and Local Examination." By November 1905 he had secured recognition by the Board of Education for the School as a Pupil Teacher Centre. His aim was clear: "I think it is very important that the Grammar School should be looked upon as the Educational centre of the district."

Meanwhile there was a field, purchased in 1904, but no pavilion. At his first Speech Day Mr Atkinson declared that this

The pavilion, one of Mr. Atkinson's first projects, was completed in 1905. It was demolished in 1964 when the School acquired its new games field.

The Preparatory Form, established by Mr Atkinson in 1905.

omission must be rectified. There would be no delay, no pleading for endowment funds; the School would raise the money, and so it did via various bazaars, concerts, lectures and plays in which the Head and his colleagues did most of the work. By 1905 the pavilion was in place at a cost of £138 8s. 11d. (together with fencing, drainage, roller, mower and water barrow) and on June 28th 1905 Sports Day was held on the field at Ben Rhydding for the first time. It was a gala occasion. While parents and friends inspected the new pavilion, "the Ilkley Council Military Band, from an elevated position on the cricket pitch, rendered a very good selection of music, which was much appreciated." The money for the pavilion was only finally paid off in 1906 "when a successful attempt to liquidate the debt was made at a dramatic performance given in St Margaret's Hall." Two one-act plays were presented, the first, "Second Thoughts," the other, more intriguingly, "Freezing a Mother-in-Law." Later provision included not only a horse to pull the roller but a stable for the horse.

There were other changes. In 1906 Mr Atkinson in effect founded the School Library, which had previously been little more than a few shelves, and established the tradition that each leaver donated a volume, which was then acknowledged in the Olicanian. He instituted the prefect system in the same year "to ensure a better control of the boys out of school" with pupils selected on a

---

→ EDUCATIONAL. ←

ILKLEY GRAMMAR SCHOOL

(FOUNDED, 1607; RECONSTITUTED, 1893).

Recognised by the Board of Education as a Secondary School. No. 10668.

STAFF :—

Headmaster:—MR. C. W. ATKINSON, M.A.,
Emmanuel College, Cambridge (Mathematical Tripos), formerly Headmaster of Normanton Grammar School.

Second Master.
MR. A. B. DOWNING, M.A.,
Open Scholar, Sidney Sussex College, Cambridge
(Natural Science Tripos).

Assistant Masters.
MR. E. DOBSON
Art Master's Certificate.

MR. H. EAMES,
London University.

MR. F. LEEDS, B.A.,
St. Catharine's College, Cambridge.

MR. W. ROBINSON, M.A.,
Victoria University.

MR. H. F. VARLEY, F.C.S.,
MR. S. W. WALKER,
London University.

MR. W. J. C. WOOD, M.A.
Christ Church, Oxford.

Preparatory Department.
MISS MURIEL WYLDE,
N.F.U. Higher Certificate.

Visiting Masters.
MR. ISAAC HURST, F.R.C.O.
MR. W. C. PLEASANCE (Woodwork).
SERGEANT INSTRUCTOR C. COXHEAD (Drill).

A Preparatory Class for Boys under 8 years of age has been formed.

The School is intended for Day Boys and Boarders who are prepared for the Local and Matriculation Examinations, and generally trained on Public School lines for Commercial or Professional life. There are 10 acres of playing fields and a Cricket Pavilion. Leaving Scholarships to the Universities.

Prospectus, List of Successes, etc., from the Headmaster or the Clerk to the Governors, JOHN W. DIXON.

A school advertisement from 1907.

house basis. The tercentenary was celebrated in 1907, the occasion marked by the founding of three Leaving Scholarships to which he personally subscribed £250. He was not averse to dipping into his own pocket. By February 1906 numbers had increased to 93, of whom 65 had been enrolled in eighteen months. This sudden increase put pressure on staffing and Mr Atkinson found himself "at his own expense employing an extra master and mistress in addition to devoting his whole time to teaching at present." Presumably the Governors responded positively to his plea that "further help would be required to do the work properly" for by December 1907 numbers had jumped again, to 137. Of these, 33 held West Riding Scholarships and 8 Free or Foundation Scholarships. Regulations determined that, to enable access to a Board of Education grant, at least 25 per cent of pupils should be 'scholarship boys'. The Governors, ever mindful of the need to maximise income, regularly tried to pin down the Board as to what lower figure it would accept without the grant being lost.

The main sports continued to be rugby and cricket. The story is told of the 1st XV travelling to an away game at Skipton, when the horse drawing their coach bolted and ran into a bank. Fortunately there were no casualties. In the early days the School had its own rifle range, on the land subsequently sold in 1903 for the Coronation Hospital. The rifle club continued, in the gymnasium for miniature-rifle shooting and also at the Ilkley range, where Baden Powell himself presented the club prizes in 1905. There was a Junior Cadet Corps but successive efforts to establish an Officer Training Corps were thwarted by the War Office. In April 1909 the Governors were involved in negotiations over the provision of a new road next to "the southern boundary of the School playing field near Sunset View." They pronounced themselves satisfied with the plans and noted that "the new road is to be known as Valley Drive."

Mr Atkinson and staff in 1907.

Left to right: Back row —, Mr Dobson, Mr Hirst, —, Mr Robinson, Mr Jennings. Front row: —, Mr Atkinson, Miss Wylde, Mr Downing.

Mr Hirst wrote the music for the School Hymn. Mr Robinson became the first Headmaster of the new Prince Henry's Grammar School in Otley in 1918.

A magnificent certificate of 1907 illustrating Town and School. It certifies that A. Thistlethwaite was honourably mentioned in General Subjects in the Midsummer Examination and is signed by Mr Atkinson.

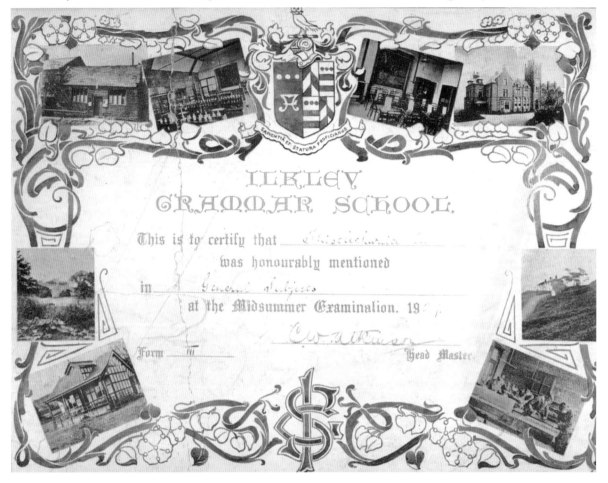

The question of local grammar school provision for girls, which was to become such a bone of contention thirty years later, first surfaced in 1905 when the Governors were invited to discuss with the West Riding "certain proposals for the provision of a Secondary School for Girls or a Dual School for Wharfedale." Their clear intention was that Ilkley Grammar should remain a boys' school and they repeated the convenient proposal from the 1902 inspection that "the provision of a Grammar School for Girls in Otley alone would for the present supply the educational requirements of the district. By this arrangement Ilkley and Otley would mutually assist each other instead of becoming antagonistic were a Grammar School for Boys erected at Otley. If a Dual Secondary School is decided on then the Governors approve of Guiseley as the most appropriate locality." Or, one might add, anywhere other than Ilkley. One can sense the relief when it was

The Obstacle Race and Tug of War at the 1911 Sports Day. The school field, purchased in 1904, was on the land now occupied by the former International Wool Secretariat building and was at that time in open countryside. The last Sports Day at the old field took place in 1962.

reported at the following meeting that the West Riding had "practically decided to provide a dual school at Guiseley, thus leaving the position of the Ilkley Grammar School unaffected."

There was another inspection in 1909. By this time there were 165 pupils, only nine of whom were boarders. As well as the Head, there were nine full-time and three part-time teachers. The report suggested that "the staff would be improved by giving higher salaries. No qualified and experienced master should be offered less than £140 per annum at this School." Its conclusion showed how things had improved since 1902:

> Under the direction of the Head Master the standard of the work done has risen steadily during the past few years and excellent progress has been made; but the School has not yet reached its full growth and should aim at the standard of a first grade school, which it just fails to reach at present. The School has made rapid progress in all respects since the last full inspection and has won for itself a well deserved reputation for good work in its own immediate neighbourhood.

This positive tone is certainly caught in the Ilkley Guide for 1911. Published by the Urban District Council, it is unashamedly effusive:

Mr Atkinson with staff and pupils in 1911.

Ilkley Grammar School is one of the most perfect institutions of its kind in the kingdom. The present school – built in 1893 – occupies a commanding position on the edge of the Moors and is equipped with laboratories, workshop, gymnasium, playing fields, lecture rooms and commodious classrooms, an extensive library and shooting range – in fact everything conducive to the tuition, recreation and healthy well-being of its students.

Another of Mr Atkinson's schemes was for the provision of a

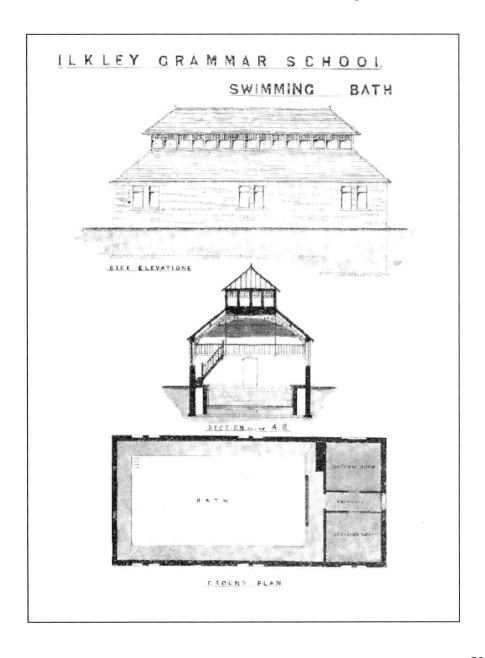

The plan for the swimming bath, opened in 1913.

swimming bath "near the present buildings and close to the eastern boundary wall." A subscription list was opened in 1911, the Head himself taking the lead by donating £25. The magazine published a draft plan, very similar to the building eventually erected, though there was a staircase and a gallery in the original scheme. The inevitable round of bazaars, concerts and lectures was organised with the aim of raising further funds. The building work was not without its problems. The foundations kept filling with water and the source was discovered to be a spring. Work was held up while experts were called in to decide whether this

Ilkley Grammar School Bazaar

WINTER CARNIVAL
AND
MODEL MARKET

TO BE HELD

AT THE SCHOOL,

On THURSDAY, NOV. 30, 1911,   To be opened
FRIDAY,   DEC.   1, „   at 3 p.m.
SATURDAY, DEC.   2, „   each day

Thursday by MRS. J. HASTINGS DUNCAN
         Chairman: J. C. NAYLOR, Esq.
Friday by THE LADY KATHARINE HARDY
         Chairman: F. H. HUMPHRIS, Esq., J.P.
Saturday by F. H. FAWKES, Esq., J.P., C.C.
         Chairman: B. M. HOOD, Esq., J.P.

Object. *To provide the School with a Swimming Bath*

Fifteen Stalls of Useful and Ornamental Goods; Refreshments, including Tea and Supper; Numerous Entertainments, Musical, Dramatic and Gymnastic; and a variety of Side Shows will be provided

ADMISSION.

THURSDAY—3 to 7 2/-, after 7 1/-.   FRIDAY— 3 to 7 1/-, after 7 6d.
SATURDAY—6d. all day.
Season Tickets 2/6.   Children and Helpers half-price.

HEMSLEY & SONS, PRINTERS, ILKLEY.

The games pavilion and the swimming bath were both provided through the kind of energetic fundraising at which Mr Atkinson excelled.

free supply could fill the bath. They decreed the flow was not sufficiently constant and a more conventional solution had to be agreed. Then, in the middle of the work, the architect, Mr Baxendall, suddenly died and negotiations had to begin with his replacement, Mr Chorley. Extra costs were incurred, for "fixed seats in the dressing boxes", for paths, and for cement on the inside walls and Mr Chorley was entrusted with the task of "constructing a cart road from the Bath to Springs Lane." Eventually, at a cost of £1,423 the work was completed and on 24th July 1912, following prayers offered by the the Vicar and the

Ilkley Grammar School
New Swimming Bath
Saturday, May 17, 1913

3.0   Opening Ceremony by MRS. H. FELL

3.30   Grand Display of Artistic and Scientific Swimming, Floating and Diving by PROFESSOR F. BOYD, Instructor to the City of Leeds Training College and leading Yorkshire Swimming Clubs, assisted by Master CHARLES BIACCHI and Master DICK BATES, School Boy Champion Swimmers of Leeds (Admission One Shilling)

3.30—5.30   Afternoon Tea

5.0   Second Display of Swimming (Admission Sixpence)

6.0   Gymnastic Display under the direction of Sergeant-Instructor COXHEAD in Gymnasium (Admission Sixpence)

7.0   Third Display of Swimming (Admission Sixpence)

8.10   Café Chantant in School Hall

singing of two hymns, the foundation stone was laid by Mrs F. B. Maufe, wife of the Chairman of the Governors. The following year, on 17th May 1913, the building was officially opened by Mrs H. Fell. Almost a hundred years later it is still in use. The magazine for Winter 1914 enthused:

The foundation stone of the swimming bath is laid by Mrs. Maufe.

> That the Swimming Bath is fulfilling its purpose was very clearly shown at the Annual Sports not only by the increased number of entries but also by the higher standard of skill displayed. The former were so numerous that preliminary trials had to be made in all of the events; the latter was particularly evident in the diving which reached a much higher level than last year. An excellent display of ornamental Swimming was given by Prof. F. Boyd, of Leeds, of high diving by Sergt. Coxhead, and of fancy diving by the boys under the direction of Sergt. Coxhead.

It was agreed that Grammar School pupils could use the bath during the summer holiday "at the price and times to be arranged by the Headmaster, that other School boys be allowed the use as a privilege during the same period at double the fee and that Old

Scholars being members of the Old Boys' Association be allowed to use the Bath at a fee of half a guinea." Perhaps the Governors needed all the money they could raise, for at the same time they were coping with an intriguing report from the Clerk "that the old boiler used for heating the premises had given way under testing by the National Boiler Company's Inspector and that it would be needful to replace it by a new boiler of greater capacity."

It was accepted that the school needed a sanatorium, as had been proposed by Mr Swann. On 6th March 1911 Dr Richardson, the Medical Officer of Health, spoke to the Governors about "the need of and use for such a building at the Ilkley Grammar School." The Headmaster "was authorised to obtain particulars as to the cost of erecting a detached building consisting of four rooms in addition to corridors, bathroom and W.C." The unfortunate Mr Baxendall, recently engaged to construct the bath, submitted plans, approved by Governors, "for the erection of a Bungalow in brick and stone on the ground at the east end of the School Buildings at present forming part of the kitchen garden." Again there were problems. The contract was agreed at a cost of £316 but Mr Baxendall had "made an error in the quantities" and moreover "the ground upon which the Bungalow was built was found to be unsuitable and in order to secure good foundations he had to go down two feet lower than he had anticipated,

Mrs. Fletcher presents the prizes at the 1912 Sports Day.

necessitating additional walling." He needed another £89. The Governors grumbled but paid up and the bungalow, later to become the Caretaker's house, was completed in 1912.

Throughout the early years of the new century there was a sense that the School, after a tentative beginning, had a clear idea of what it wanted to achieve and was playing an increasingly important role in the local community. The magazine embodied this new-found confidence by increasing in size. It began to include photography, with pictures of rugby and cricket teams, of the new pavilion, of boys in the school workshop and of all eight members of the Preparatory Form. As well as chronicling the more conventional aspects of life such as Speech Day, Empire Day and what must have seemed interminable concerts, there are sports results, including some disarmingly frank appraisals of team members. Then there are the more unusual activities:

> At the beginning of term there was a good deal of skating, and in consequence School was dismissed half-an-hour earlier than usual on three occasions in order to allow more time to be spent on the ice. (1902)

This risky business presumably took place on the tarn. The school pigeon cote was also giving problems:

> The Pigeon Syndicate has had very hard times again. At the beginning of the term they re-stocked the pigeon cote. Alas! Disaster followed disaster. What with cats, thieves, and other outside marauders, there is only one poor unfortunate left. In despair the Syndicate has turned to rabbits for consolation. The mother unfortunately slept on four of the young ones, and they were afterwards buried amidst universal gloom. (1903)

There are reports of 'expeditions', at first local (to Malham Cove, the Lakes and even down a coal mine), later further afield, and eventually abroad. There is news that the School has purchased a husky dog for Captain Scott's ill-fated 1911 Antarctic expedition. There are staff comings and goings; the Winter Term 1906 issue mentions the arrival of Mr Robinson, who left in 1918 to become the first Headmaster of the re-opened Prince Henry's Grammar School in Otley and of Miss Wylde, a much-loved teacher who spent her entire career at Ilkley until her death in 1930. In 1905 Mr Atkinson introduced the words of a 'School and Holiday Hymn' which were then set to music by Isaac Hirst, the Music Master and organist at the Parish Church. With its resounding refrain, "Floruit, Floret, Floreat" ("It flourished, it flourishes, may it go on flourishing") it became the School Song for generations of Olicanians:

Once more to part, our mother,
Thy children round thee stand,
For thee with one another
Uniting heart and hand.
For thee we lift our voices,
For thee we shout our song,
For thee each tongue rejoices,
That swell our vocal throng.

Chorus: *Floruit, Floret, Floreat,*
Olicana's children cry,
Through good or ill,
God guard thee still,
Our boast through years gone by.

So let our lives, grown olden
With many a winter wan,
Be wreathed with memories golden
Of days for ever gone;
Of mind and arm excelling,
Of work with conquest crowned,
Of walls our triumph telling
And thy dear name renowned.

Chorus: *Floruit, Floreat, etc.*

In 1907 the house system was instituted, with the prosaic Blue, Black, Red and Yellow. In the same year there was an outbreak of mumps "which, in spite of every precaution, spread to such an extent that it was decided on March 1st to close the school." The prizes at Speech Day in 1909 were presented by local author Halliwell Sutcliffe. There was a growing interest in the School's history. In 1907 there was an article about it in the magazine, accompanied by the famous photo of the old building on Skipton Road. This prompted a terse response from John Beanlands, who had been a pupil there: "It was known as the Grammar School, but the one thing they taught least was grammar."

Another tradition was established among Old Boys of gathering around the gas lamp at the top of Brook Street after their Annual Dinner to sing 'Auld Lang Syne'. As the Old Olicanian of 1910 makes clear, these were hearty but not always orderly occasions:

Leaving behind us then, the thick, viscous, impenetrable

Once more to part.

SCHOOL HYMN.

Isaac Hirst, F.R.C.O.

The School Hymn. In 1905 Mr Atkinson's words were set to music by Isaac Hurst.

ONCE MORE TO PART.

Through good or ill . . God guard thee still, . . Our boast through years gone

After last verse only.

rall.

by. by, . . . Our boast through years gone by.

rall.

2.

The summer winds, returning,
Have called us far away,
Where tender hearts are yearning
To grace our holiday;
Yet girt with every pleasure,
With lips and fancy free,
Still chiefest may we treasure
A loyal thought for thee.
Floruit, Floret, Floreat, &c.

3.

Nor let the thoughts of sadness
Within their bosoms swell,
Who 'mid these sounds of gladness
Bid boyhood's scenes farewell;
Their past shall live for ever,
Their names be ever dear,
Nor life nor death can sever
God's ties of blessing here.
Floruit, Floret, Floreat, &c.

4.

So let our lives, grown olden
With many a winter wan,
Be wreathed with memories golden
Of days for ever gone;
Of mind and arm excelling,
Of work with conquest crowned,
Of walls our triumph telling
And thy dear name renowned.
Floruit, Floret, Floreat, &c.

(3)

*Cricket Team
1908:*

Back Row l to r:
W.M. Gummer
C.E. Dove
W.W. Green
R.F. Cobby
J.F. Winterburn
F.G. Pearce
E.Earnshaw

Front Row l to r:
L. Farrar
J.M. King
*E.F. Wilkinson
(Captain)*
*T.A. Holroyd
(Vice-Captain)*
W.S.Smeeth

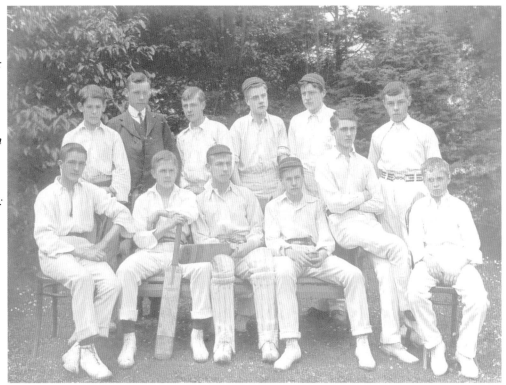

*Rugby 1st XV
1913-14:*

Back Row l to r:
Dove,
Breffit,
Lupton,
Brownlow,
Bartle,
Lickfold,
Burns

Centre l to r:
Russell,
Gledhill,
Cobby (Captain)
Sellers,
Akeroyd

Front Row l to r:
White,
Moxon,
Atkinson,
Hardaker

atmosphere of the heated room, we passed out into the cool freshness and purity of the rain-washed air, and beneath a clear, starry sky, joined hands in an unbroken ring, and sang the songs of true and lasting friendship. We also bellowed other songs, careering round the lamp post at the head of Brook Street, and not till half-past eleven had struck did we finally break up, and with much hand-shaking and many good wishes retire for a well-earned rest.

The headship of Mr Atkinson had been, thus far and in the spirit of the times, an Edwardian heyday. The School was thriving, traditions were being laid down and there was among pupils a camaraderie which lived on beyond their days at Cowpasture Road. And yet these young men, revelling in the innocent joy of their annual reunion, little knew that in a few short years their well-ordered world would be torn apart with unimaginable savagery.

At War

So much has been written in the public press and elsewhere of the reasons why Great Britain has taken up arms in this, the most terrible and gigantic war of all times, that it would serve no purpose to reiterate here those reasons. It will be sufficient, perhaps, if we confine ourselves to stating briefly how we have been affected, and what share we are taking in our Country's hour of need.

Thus the 1914 Winter Term Olicanian ominously announced the outbreak of hostilities. The School was immediately involved. Already, with the war only a few months old, 121 Old Olicanians had "answered the call and joined the colours." The sense that, in these early days, the war was considered a bit of an adventure is evident in the admission that "some of the 'Sixth' have tried to pass the Recruiting Officer who, while commending them on their physique, has rejected them because of their apparent youthfulness." Other boys gave part of their pocket money to various relief funds, while most in the Upper School turned up for voluntary drill. There were Belgian refugees living locally. There were "stirring addresses from our Headmaster from time to time and the patriotic service, including the reading of the Roll of Honour, every Monday morning." Many Olicanians wrote to Mr Atkinson about their experiences in the war and each night he sat down to write letters back to them.

The casualties began in 1915. The first was Colin Cattley who had left in 1898. He was "a victim of one of the most diabolical acts in the annals of civilisation, the sinking of the Lusitania by the Germans." He had become a rancher in Canada; when he died he was on his way home to see his mother for the first time in five years. Very quickly the school magazines were full of additions to the Roll of Honour of those who had joined up, and, tragically, more deaths.

At the same time there began to arrive letters from far-flung places. Lieut. J. H. Mawson wrote of war's contrasts from the Gallipoli Peninsula:

We have been here for nearly three weeks now – a lovely country, plenty of sunshine and flowers, plenty of work and food and fun, and plenty of excitement. Have been mostly on road-making, trench digging and barbed wire erecting. Road-making consists mostly of disinterring or re-burying Turks – a gruesome business. My section has unfortunately lost rather heavily. Am myself a bearded and unwashed savage and cave dweller.

C. Hobbs on HMS Lookout was breezily optimistic:

By the way, we came across a 'Zep' the other day but she was not quite near enough for any of us to have any sport in bringing her down. You can tell them all at School that the 'Lads in Blue' are quite cheerful and looking forward to the High Sea Fleet of Germany coming out for an airing.

Private H. Wilkinson reported from the trenches:

I think this morning I hit my first German. His lordship was working on their parapet which is four hundred yards off. He suddenly disappeared from view after I fired.

The horrors of war were never far away. I.F. Burns wrote:

True, when the man next to me got a sniper's bullet through his face, an inch below the eyes, one was brought back with a jerk to the reality of the situation, but it was not until the shells came over that things became a bit too lively. There were only six of them and they were nothing to what we have had since, but to us novices the scream which proclaimed their arrivals, the crash of explosion and the subsequent hurtling round of divers fragments was rather trying, especially after the decapitation of a sergeant by one.

In the midst of all this the School suffered a severe loss closer to home. From her son Kenneth's letters we know that in November 1915 Mrs Atkinson was ill with influenza. The following month he is enquiring after his father: "I hope Father is better, & will be absolutely well when I get home." It was not to be. Mr Atkinson died on 11th December 1915; he was 45 years old. A brass memorial tablet was placed on the wall of St Margaret's Church, where he had been a warden and whither he brought Grammar School boys every Sunday morning. He was remembered with enormous affection. The school memorial was a library and, perhaps curiously, a bath area in the old pavilion, dedicated in 1924. Over the door of the bathroom were printed some verses written by an Old Boy, Eric Wilkinson, which concluded:

For his stirring call and his grand old rule –
That heart and courage must never fail –
Will live as long as the grey stone school
Looks out on the broad green vale.

Eric Wilkinson himself typifies the promising young lives brought to an untimely end. He excelled at school, both at sport and academically. He studied Engineering at Leeds University before returning as a junior master. Before the war he had published "Sunrise Dreams and Other Poems." When war broke out he joined up and, because he had already served in the University OTC, he was commissioned in the West Yorkshire Regiment. He was sent to France where, "for conspicuous gallantry and coolness" in carrying a wounded soldier over No Man's Land at night, he was awarded the Military Cross. Subsequently he was bayoneted and gassed, and then wounded by a bomb at Thiepval on 1st July 1916. After spending some time in hospital he returned to France, where he was again gassed, losing his sight for three days. His death is recorded in the Olicanian of Autumn 1917:

The end came on Oct. 9 last, when he fell, leading the first wave of the attack on some part of Passchendaele Ridge. Amid the sea of mud he became separated from his men and was last seen making single-handed for the German lines, whilst his men vainly endeavoured to keep in touch with him. Truly a hero's death.

Capt. Eric F. Wilkinson M.C.

Eric Wilkinson was twenty six years old. His name is commemorated on the plaque in the Library and there is a memorial to him in Ben Rhydding Methodist Church.

One night in the autumn of 1915 Lt. Wilkinson, in his Flanders dug-out, had received a letter from Mr Atkinson enclosing the rugby fixture card for the season. This inspired him to write his most famous poem, "The Song of the Fixture Card", subsequently anthologised in "The Muse in Arms" in 1917. It begins:

You came by last night's mail
To my strange little mud-built house,
At a time when the blues were on my trail
And I'd little to do but grouse.
For the world seemed a-swim with ooze,
With everything going wrong,
And though I knew that we couldn't lose,
Yet the end of it all seemed long.
The sandbag bed felt hard,
And exceedingly cold the rain,
But you sang to me, little green card,
And gave me courage again;
For at sight of the old green back,
And the dear familiar crest,
I was off and away on memory's track,
Where Rombold's Moor stands bleak and black
And the plaintive curlews nest.

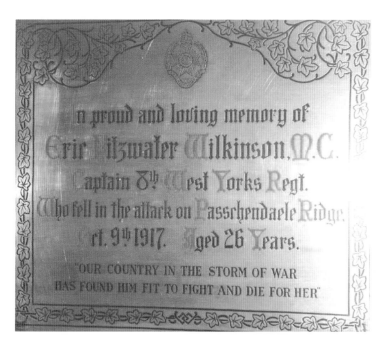

The memorial plaque to Eric Wilkinson in Ben Rhydding Methodist Church.

Mike Dixon

By kind permission of Ben Rhydding Methodist Church.

In the Summer 1915 issue of the Olicanian Norman Tennant described the view as he gazed across Northern France:

At the present moment I'm reclining on a bank of earth at one of our observation stations – a big pear tree – a little to the right of the battery, and, from the top of this one may see the country for miles around. On nearly three sides lie the trenches about 1000 yards from here, and the reports of the rifles can be heard distinctly. Every now and then one hears the sudden bursts of rifle and machine-gun fire as an aeroplane passes low over the trenches, and then the anti-aircraft guns – or 'Archibalds,' as they are called – begin to speak, fairly surrounding the machine with little white puffs of smoke which hang together and drift in the wind long after the shells have burst, so that an aeroplane's course is plainly marked across the sky by these little smoke clouds.

In 1988 Norman Tennant, then aged 93, wrote to the School, remembering Eric Wilkinson:

Captain Eric Fitzwater Wilkinson M.C. was School Captain in the pre-1914 days when I was a very shy and bewildered 'new boy' starting my life at Ilkley Grammar School. Our paths rarely crossed but I remember meeting Eric quite by chance in a quiet part of the battlefront in 1917 shortly before he was reported 'missing' later that year during the long, savage series of attacks on Passchendaele. It was due to a re-awakened interest in his poems that I decided to try to locate his grave, if any. The War Graves Commission were able to tell me where Eric's name was engraved in a huge decorative wall commanding a view over the vast sea of gravestones in Tyne Cot Cemetery in the Ypres Salient. I travelled to France last month for the 70th anniversary of the Armistice Ceremony at the Menin Gate in Ypres. The next day I moved up to Tyne Cot and laid a wreath at the foot of the stone on which is engraved the name of Captain Eric Fitzwater Wilkinson.

Norman Tennant at Tyne Cot Cemetery in November 1988. He is standing beside the wall on which is engraved the name of Eric Fitzwater Wilkinson. The message on the wreath reads: "Capt. E.F. Wilkinson. An Old Olicanian remembers you, Eric."

Enclosed was a photo of Norman standing in front of the section of the wall at Tyne Cot on which Eric Wilkinson's name is inscribed.

Meanwhile, life at school moved on and the new Head, Norman Lewis Frazer, Head of

Batley Grammar School, was appointed in 1916. His was not an easy task, taking over from the much-loved Mr Atkinson, who had remained in contact with so many of the staff and former pupils now on active service. Moreover the war was showing no sign of ending and the depressing list of fatalities continued. In autumn 1916 there was news of eleven deaths and in summer 1917 a further ten. The School did what it could to support the war effort. It had its own War Savings branch and by 1917 1045 certificates had been purchased, yielding £810. Potatoes were grown in the school grounds and in one year 22 cwts. were harvested. For several years the School supported three prisoners of war, sending parcels each week, and pupils were rewarded with fortnightly postcards and the occasional letter. Tin foil was collected and in one year 165 lbs. were sent in, realising £2, while in response to the government's appeal for horse-chestnuts, 3 cwts. were collected and despatched. Ernest Rayner (1915-18) remembered the School Cadet Corps, which used to parade in the field at the back of the swimming baths. The boys were trained by Sgt. Baker, a veteran of the Boer War. They did army drill with dummy wooden guns and rifle practice with proper rifles on a range in Easby Drive near the railway embankment and at an indoor range on Bolling Road.

Letters continued to pour in from all corners of the world. W.S. Walker, a former master, wrote from the Cameroon:

I should want more than a letter to describe to you the ripping journey I'm having. Troubles there are, of course – for instance when a carrier falls down and breaks all your crockery or one of your servants gets lost – but they are nothing. I am passing close to pagan cannibals now, but no excitement.

Raymond Sawdon reported "from somewhere in the desert":

My first visit to the Pyramids was rather a disappointment. I expected them to be much bigger. But since then I am glad they are no bigger because I had to climb the exterior, and do some signalling work from the top, and it's half an hour's climb.

There was a poignancy about Private G.F.S. Brownlow's letter from the trenches:

We are doing fine work along this line as you will perhaps see from the papers. Our chaps are expecting to go over the parapet at the Germans any day – we are only waiting for the word. I only wish I had a school chum to fight with me through the h--l we have been in. We go into a hot corner for 18 to 24 days when we are only about 30 yards away. Bien des choses à tous mes amis.

The end of the war in November 1918 was greeted with a mixture of relief and deep sadness, for although hostilities were now at an end, there were, ironically, more deaths reported in the Olicanian in Autumn 1918 than in any other single term. Indeed it was not until 1919 that the final fatalities were known.

As life began to return to normality, it was agreed that a War Memorial in the form of a lectern, designed by Frank Brangwyn RA and paid for by subscription, should be placed in the School Hall. On Saturday July 3rd 1920 Mr Swann returned to unveil it. In doing so he spoke of the losses suffered and the bravery of those who had laid down their lives:

Few indeed if any Schools have suffered greater losses in proportion to their numbers than the Ilkley Grammar School – stern proof, if such were needed, that her sons stood always where the danger was greatest.

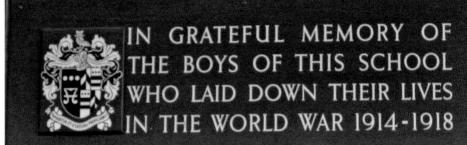

The First World War Memorial in the School Library.

IN GRATEFUL MEMORY OF THE BOYS OF THIS SCHOOL WHO LAID DOWN THEIR LIVES IN THE WORLD WAR 1914-1918

SAMUEL ERIC DITCHFIELD
GEORGE CORRALL TURNER
ALFRED WOOD
ERIC F. WILKINSON
JOSEPH DURRANS
FRED NORMAN WOOD
JAMES G. HUTCHINSON
MAURICE DACRE
BASIL STAINFORTH MANN
JAMES ANTHONY LINCEY
GEORGE VYVIAN GREEN
THOMAS H. WHITAKER
WILLIAM H. STOWE
ERNEST H. ARMITAGE
ALBERT HOWES
GORDON M. DUNCAN
RALF L. MACKRIDGE
HAROLD HOUSEMAN
ERIC HARVEY CORNWELL
NORMAN MULLER
HUGH McALISTER A. BLACK
GEOFFREY SKIRROW

JOHN ROWLAND NELSON
LESLIE G. HUTCHINSON
JOHN CUTHBERT BROWN
BRIAN DACRE
HAROLD HIRST
GODFREY MICHAEL SMITH
THOMAS HORSMAN
AMOS CLARKSON
EDGAR EARNSHAW
CECIL M. COLEMAN
CLARENCE D. BOOTHMAN
GILBERT FOSTER HADDOCK
ROY COWLING
HENRY SCOTT CRYER
ERNEST CHAPMAN
EDWARD C. WINTLE
NOEL WILLIAM LITTLE
GEORGE C. WHITAKER
ARTHUR BASIL LEE
LEONARD FOSTER
GERALD HARMER
REGINALD H. BUTTERFIELD

NINIAN HORREL BARR
LISTER HOLROYD
HAROLD C. PONTING
HENRY J. GREENHILL
ALFRED MACKENZIE
GEOFFREY PONTING
BERNARD N. HARVEY
ERNEST C. LANSDALE
GEORGE ALLAN EXLEY
HARRY JOSEPH IDESON
ALLAN MOISLEY
FREDERICK ROBINSON
HENRY COWARD (MASTER)
JACK HAROLD BRYANT
CECIL ARTHUR CRYER
PHILIP FLETCHER DIXON
ALFRED LUCAS
CHARLES LISTER
ARTHUR REGINALD DEAN
ISLAY FERRIER BURNS
WILLIAM SUTTON SMEETH
ERIC WILKINSON KNOWLES

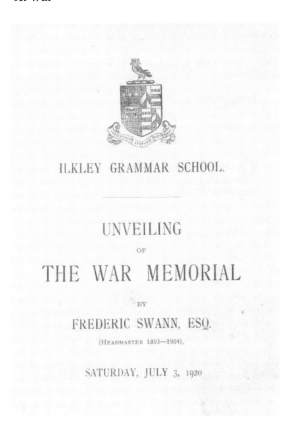

The War Memorial, a lectern designed by Frank Brangwyn R.A. and unveiled by Mr Swann in July 1920.

Many of them, as I well know, were gentle and loving souls to whom strife and bloodshed were abhorrent. War was not their trade. They were lovers of peace, and engaged in peaceful pursuits. They went to battle from no love of fighting but simply because they were impelled by the strongest sense of duty and patriotism. They felt they could do no other. They did not stay to analyse the motive, but we who perhaps knew them better than they knew themselves, we know that the root impulse was the love of home, of kith and kin, of what was right and just and true and honourable, that drove them to the task they hated. They went because they believed that if they failed to go our Country would no longer be a fit dwelling place for those they held dearest and best. Thus they unconsciously displayed that love than which none is greater – that a man lay down his life for his friend.

The School and the local community had indeed suffered grievously, for no fewer than sixty six names were thus commemorated.

Boys - and Girls

The Great War was over. The School had commemorated its dead, though, like the rest of the country, it continued to mourn their passing, especially at the newly-introduced Armistice Day ceremony. In Ilkley, as elsewhere, it was a time to begin to look forward.

The Prospectus for 1920 paints a broad picture of the School. It was clearly casting its net far and wide:

> The Ilkley Grammar School is administered under a Scheme of the Charity Commissioners as a First Grade School for Boarders and Day-Boys, and is conducted as a recognised Secondary School under the Board of Education. The School, which is capable of accommodating 200 boys, is healthily situated about 500 feet above sea level and is close to the Moors. It is within five minutes' walk of the Ilkley Railway Station, which is within easy reach of Leeds and Bradford, and is easily accessible for day scholars from Burley, Menston, Guiseley, Otley, Addingham etc.; also from the North of England by the N.E. Railway via Harrogate and Otley; from Lancashire via Hellifield and Skipton; and from the South by the Midland and G.N. Railways via Leeds. The buildings, which were erected in 1893 and enlarged in 1898, are fitted with every modern convenience and appliance for effective instruction. The Sanitary arrangements, to which special care and attention have been given, have received the Certificate of the Inspector of the Bradford Sanitary Association. The Class Rooms are lofty, well lighted and carefully ventilated; in winter the rooms and corridors are heated throughout by means of hot water. The new wing contains Chemical and Physical Laboratories, Art Rooms, a Gymnasium, Carpenter's Workshop and covered playground. The Head Master's House adjoins the School; there is accommodation for 40 boarders, and ample provision for isolation, in case of illness, in the recently erected bungalow. In the rear of the School there is a large playground and field, in addition to which there is a five acre field for Cricket and Football at Ben Rhydding. A spacious covered Swimming Bath has recently been erected

at a cost of £1,600.

In July 1920 there was an inspection, the first since 1909, and the ensuing report gives a more detailed assessment. Numbers had increased from 167 in 1914 to 208, this in spite of the fact that schools had opened at Otley and Guiseley. Indeed there was some overcrowding of boarders. The report gives the "Class in life from which the Boys are drawn." The figures are percentages:

Professional - - - -	20
Farmers - - - - -	2
Wholesale Traders - - -	20
Retail Traders and Contractors -	18
Clerks and Commercial Agents -	15
Public Service - - - -	4
Domestic Service - - -	4
Artisans - - - - -	12
Occupation, none or unknown -	5

There is concern that "the average length of school life beyond the age of 12" is only 2 years and 4 months:

Considering the class from which the boys are largely drawn, the length of school life is disappointingly short. Some boys have entered the School too late and many more have left too young. Both features are partly due to the high proportion of residents whose stay in the area is short.

Tuition fees varied from £9 9s. for 6 – 8 year olds to £14 for those over 12. Some subjects incurred an extra charge, Piano £4 14s. 6d., Violin £7 17s. 6d. and Woodwork 10s. Boarding fees varied from £42 to £60. Accommodation was again a problem, with "school premises now taxed to their utmost capacity. There is a deficiency in classroom accommodation which necessitates Forms being taken in the hall and in the boarders' day room." Life was little better for staff: "The only room available as a common room for Masters is totally inadequate; the Mistresses have only the Library for this purpose." Nevertheless the general tone of the report is positive, as are the individual subject comments, though, intriguingly, in Physical Exercise "'Hollow back' was very noticeable among many of the classes and the carriage of the head often left much to be desired." The report concluded:

The recent history of the School has been one of steady progress on which the Governors and Headmaster are to be congratulated. Its growing reputation is attracting more and more boarders from the West Riding and places beyond. The standard of work needs raising at the top if the School is to reach first grade rank. The recent progress of the School, backed as it is by a long tradition and an established position, should bring this goal within nearer reach.

Soon the number of boys had reached 225, of whom 52 were boarders. These were accommodated in three houses: School House, which had twenty eight boarders, and two houses run as private ventures by staff, a hostel in Wheatley Road where there were sixteen and Craig End Lodge where there were eight. There were fourteen full-time staff and two part-time, for Woodwork and Singing. Though there were grants from the Board of Education and the West Riding, the bulk of the School's income still came from fees and its own funds and it appeared that it was just about paying its way. There were now fifty eight free places, twenty five from the West Riding and thirty three from the Foundation Scholarship scheme.

Norman Lewis Frazer, Headmaster from 1916 to 1933.

There are several accounts of school life at this time. Mr Frazer was notorious for his strict discipline and was feared by the boys. One day a boy 'back-heeled' the form room door. As a punishment he had to spend the whole of the following afternoon 'back-heeling' the door. There is no record of the state of boy or door when he'd finished but Mr Frazer passed the afternoon watching the punishment unfold. If a parent complained, Mr Frazer's usual response was, "If you don't like my methods, remove your son!" Wilfred Powell, who joined in 1916, recalls:

Mr Frazer was very strict. I remember fooling around and accidentally breaking a window with my head. Mrs Frazer bandaged me up and Mr Frazer insisted I mend the window, so I did it with my brother and a friend. There was plenty of caning. If you didn't know an answer, you stood on the seat. If you still didn't know, you stood on the desk, and if you still didn't know, you were put on the window sill. I remember one lad who was lame. When he went swimming you could see weals on his legs. Miss Wylde was furious and stormed off to do battle with Mr Frazer for caning a cripple. 'Ike' Hurst wrote the school song. I remember a lad next to him singing flat. He got blamed and was sent for a caning.

Elizabeth Howard's father, Harry Kirby, was a boarder in the 1920s. He recalled going to Burley with friends when they were very hungry and calling at a farmhouse where they bought a turnip for a ha'penny then cut it up with a pen knife and shared it round. Food was in short supply and most of the boarders tried to persuade their parents to send parcels. For a very special treat Mrs Frazer would make a rabbit pie.

Rob Olver was a pupil from 1915 to 1922. He was a talented cartoonist and his drawings appeared regularly in the Olicanian. He tells this story:

A senior boarder from Lincolnshire decided to take part in a local grouse shoot. He collected six juniors to act as beaters and set out for the lower reaches of Ilkley Moor, having, like David of old, selected smooth round pebbles from Backstone Beck. He scorned the use of a sling or catapult as he was an excellent cricketer. One luckless grouse, which had evaded the real shoot, was located in the heather. As instructed, the youngsters slowly walked the grouse to the selected killing ground, a low bare ridge behind which the hunter concealed himself. As the grouse's head appeared over the ridge, one well-aimed missile killed it instantly. The corpse was carried in triumph back to school. The news spread quickly and, as usual, soon reached the Headmaster. Mr Frazer was furious and at the next morning assembly spoke at length about the boy's "disgusting, unsportsmanlike behaviour." He followed this up by sending the marksman plus grouse to a local J.P., who owned the shooting rights on Rombalds Moor, with instructions to make an apology. He was received by the gentleman in question, invited in for tea, asked for full details of his mini-drive, thanked for the still-edible grouse and complimented on his splendid 'shot'.

Ernest Rayner remembers learning to swim in the baths. "Miss Wylde used to hold us up with a cloth belt around the chest and walked down the side of the pool while one tried to make attempts at swimming. This gave one confidence to enter the water." He also recalls a young man coming up Cowpasture Road from Hartley's confectioners at morning break with iced buns which he sold for a penny each.

Alan Thompson (1917-23) tells a story about Mr Lovelock, who taught Games and History:

A class dealing with the dissolution of the monasteries was once taken to Bolton Abbey to inspect the remains of the Augustinian Priory there. Shortly after Lovelock had begun his discourse and tour of the ruins, the party was joined by several tourists – including two Americans. When the tour was over, one of the Americans came up to Lovelock and said, "Say guy, you sure know your stuff," at the same time thrusting a half crown into his hand – a gift which Lovelock acknowledged with a touch of his hat and later transferred to a charity collection box kept in the hall of the school.

A feature of the staff at this time was its stability. Of those listed in the 1920 Prospectus, five, Messrs. Eames, Bartle, Evans, Lovelock and Ebdon were still teaching in 1940. As ever, pupils quickly latched on to eccentricity and Wilfred Powell remembers a rhyme about Mr Dobson, the Art Master, who had problems with

Mr Frazer and staff in the mid-1920s..

Left to Right: Back Row: Mr Eames, Mr Nuttall, Mr Lovelock, Mr Ebdon, Mr Barratt, Mr Simpson, Mr Bartle.
Front Row: Mrs Scott, Miss Wylde, Mr Evans, Mr Frazer, Mr Dobson, Miss Brigg, Miss Yeadon.

the letter 'h':

> *The Honourable Hedward is my name*
> *Hart my Hoccupation*
> *Richmond is my 'appy 'ome*
> *Hand 'ell my destination.*

When Mr Dobson retired in 1929 he had taught at the School for thirty six years; he was the last of the "Swann men". An inspection report of 1927 paid tribute to the quality of the staff "which taken as a body, is an unusually good one. The proportion of teachers of outstanding capacity is exceptionally high, and it contains much less than its normal share of weaker elements." Overall it was a positive report: "Since the last Inspection the School has made steady progress and in every department of its life and energies the aim is high and the achievement good." There was one slight cloud on the horizon; numbers were down, from 239 in 1922 to 221 in 1926. It appeared at the time to be a minor issue but it would become a major one in the coming decade. In particular, the number of boarders began to fall quite dramatically, perhaps due to the worsening economic situation, until by 1932 there were none at all.

The pages of the Olicanian continue to chronicle termly life. The Editorial, the School Notes, the house and team reports, the account of the annual Speech Day, news of various societies, the literary efforts, even the termly inter-house 'Intellectual Championship' – the overall pattern changes little from year to year. Occasionally characters and events jump from the page. In 1925 G.K.Chesterton was the guest at the Speech Day. As he toured the School, a working model of a military catapult caught his eye. Apparently "he made covetous reference to it" in his address, "whereupon a boy was immediately sent up to school and the model was presented there and then to the Great Man who, to the unbounded delight of the assembled gathering, played with it throughout the remainder of the proceedings." His visit, moreover, gave rise to another singular event, recounted by Norman Salmon:

> While staying in Ilkley he went for a stroll. He carried a sword-stick. A local constable observed him, picturesque in sombrero-like hat and caped overcoat, making passes with his sword-stick at a tree. Thinking he was some odd character from a local institution, the constable took him into close, though very temporary, arrest.

Another character made his appearance in 1919 with the announcement: "Great news! We are to have Robert Peel for a

Rugby Team
1920 - 21

Back Row l to r:
A.S. Keighley,
E.H. Walker,
S.B Johnson,
E.R.Hall,
H. Cooper,
A.C.Robertshaw.
E.C.Hobbs

Centre l to r:
C.W.Hellewell,
Hobbs,
F.R.Stansfield,
W.T. Oliver,
J. Dawson (Capt)
R.H. Olver,
D. MacDougall

Front Row l to r:
J. Turner,
J.R. MacDougall

Cricket Team
1928

Back Row l to r:
E.H. Bland
W.D. Boyle
G.T. Greenhalgh
J. Williamson
A. Hutton
M.G. Crawshaw

Front Row l to r:
E.L. Keighley
G.F.D. Higgins
(Vice Captain)
Mr Girling
W.D. Thornton
(Captain)
C.E. Triffitt
R.S. White

cricket coach. It will take some living up to!" The post-war standard of cricket was relatively poor but "with the aid of Bobby Peel the future is more promising." Bobby Peel was in fact an old Yorkshire and England spin bowler, though he had not appeared in the county's colours for over twenty years. On that occasion, in the words of cricket historian Don Mosey, "a spectacularly inebriated interlude on the field at Bramall Lane left Lord Hawke [the Yorkshire captain] with no option but dismissal." Some say Peel set off to bowl in the wrong direction, others that he "spoke out of turn to his lordship." Anyhow, he went off to play in the Lancashire League and by the end of the war, aged over 60, was enjoying a late career as a school cricket coach. However his name appears only the once. The reason may be not too hard to find. Wilfred Powell recalled many years later, "Robert Peel took us for coaching at the cricket field. He used to drink behind the pavilion."

At the same time, the new technology of the day was generating enthusiasm. As early as 1921 comes the announcement that "we are setting up a Wireless installation." Two years later the excitement is palpable: "The School Wireless is now really working; a new valve and transformer have enabled us to get London and Manchester quite clearly. We are open to receive offers of a 'loud speaker' from any fellow enthusiast." Soon there is a Wireless Society, "which is showing a good deal of initiative although it is not yet a term old. We were all invited to a Whist Drive after Junior Sports, and spent a very enjoyable evening, although we made too much noise to allow the radio music to be audible." By the end of the year the Society has Mr Frazer as its President and is clearly up and running:

> At last we have a respectable school "wireless." Our progress, though slow, has been sure. We installed a single valve set which, thanks to generous donations, has grown to a three valve set. Broadcasting has been received practically every evening this term, except of course when the accumulators were run down, or when minor repairs were being carried out.

The nucleus of a Scout group was mentioned in the 1920 Report. By 1924 it had become the 5th Ilkley (Grammar School) Troop. It was founded by Mr Elliott and did not cease activities until 1958. During the twenties and thirties it enjoyed a vigorous life, due largely to the energetic support given by Gray Sutcliffe, an Old Olician. It held camps, including two in Belgium, the first recorded instances of school parties visiting the continent, it won a variety of trophies and boasted a Kazoo Dance Band.

In 1924 the School was saddened to hear of the death of Mr Swann. Following his career as a barrister, he had joined the staff of the Times. He held a special place in the affection of the oldest of the Old Boys – there was a tradition at their Dinner that the Swann Boys stood up and greeted each other – and was a regular visitor to Yorkshire, for he had a house at Appletreewick. The tribute paid was heartfelt and sincere:

> A schoolboy is usually somewhat of a rough diamond but he generally has a shrewd knack of "sizing up" a master, and

Invitation to the Old Boys' Association Dinner in November 1919.

his judgement of a master in later days is usually a very accurate one; and in this case the unanimous judgement of the Old Boys of the School is that Mr Swann was "one of the very best."

As always, little items of news lend immediacy. Here is rugby practice in 1922:

The rugger practice in the school field on Friday is still held and on Monday there is another practice or "bear fight" to give it its proper name. We turn out in "footer togs" and gym shoes, and "scrag" each other mercilessly for half-an-hour or so – regardless of who happens to have the ball. However it is an excellent method of keeping fit, and is particularly enjoyed by certain IVth Form ruffians, who delight in pulling Mr Elliott to pieces.

The "Here And There" feature in the Old Olicanian has an air of studied insouciance:

Three Rob Olver cartoons from the Olicanian 1919 - 22.

The two Bamptons have been demobilised. One of them was captured at Kut and has been staying in Turkey; he is going to take up tea planting again in India. The other was in Baghdad.

F. Chippendale has won some high honour in the world of Art.

Jim Eric Turner is doing well in Japan, quite safe.

'Pongo' Smith has passed an exam of some importance in the merchant service.

There are lots more in a similar vein, many of them sporting intriguing nicknames. The likes of 'Squidge' Box, 'Minnow' Milnes, 'Tishy' Arnott, 'Corpus' Oddy and the memorable 'Feet' Wilkinson stalk these pages. There is a camaraderie, interspersed with the termly and increasingly desperate pleas from the Treasurer to those members who have fallen hopelessly behind with their subscriptions.

In 1930 an Old Boy recalled the tensions between the boarders, the day boys and the 'train' boys who travelled in from Otley, Burley and Addingham:

"Train boys" – the words in the mouth of a boarder or day boy had an insulting flavour which led to many a rousing scrap. There were occasional fierce alliances between train boys and boarders, both passionate minorities with a large but rather disorganised common enemy, and at such times plans would be made by the joint conspirators during the lunch hour, and an ambush laid at the bottom gate of the school – the top gate being too near the headmaster's house! – to trap the day boys as they returned to afternoon school. These battles were particularly frequent in times of snow, and after a heavy bout of snowballing it was a nice point how best to retreat upfield at a sufficient pace when the bell rang for school without turning one's back recklessly on the enemy and receiving an icy douche in the neck. This division of the school into sections – so much more fundamental and dynamic than the artificial though excellent divisions of the house system – resulted not only in those sudden feuds and equally sudden alliances, but a healthy rivalry both in the classroom and on the playing field.

In June 1930 the Yorkshire Post ran an article which showed how widely the School cast its net:

Under the leadership of Mr Swann and his successors, Mr Atkinson and Mr Frazer, Ilkley Grammar School has gained a reputation extending far beyond the county border, and attracted scholars from the Colonies and all parts of the British Isles. One of the best athletes of pre-war days was from South America and, more recently, the school 'Rugger' team has been strengthened by a rare infusion of Scottish vigour in the forward line.

At times national events intruded. The 1926 General Strike meant there were problems for the "train boys" which were solved by bringing them to school on a lorry. The Old Boys, as might be anticipated, had little time for the strikers and boasted that "at the swearing-in of the Ilkley Specials, every other fellow seemed to be an Old Boy." There is news of one having "a hot five minutes

Programme for the Old Olicanians' Association Twenty-Sixth Anniversary.

OLD OLICANIANS' ASSOCIATION

Programme of the Twenty=Sixth Anniversary,

1926

Saturday, November 27th

9 30 a.m.	Golf Match, Ilkley Moor Golf Club.
2 30 p.m.	Football Match, School v. Old Boys. *(Old Boys' Team jerseys provided on the field)*
6 15 p.m.	Annual Meeting at Troutbeck Hydro. You are urgently requested to attend.
7 0 p.m.	ANNUAL DINNER at TROUTBECK HYDRO. Tickets 6/- each. (Morning Dress.)

By reverting once more to Troutbeck, which is now under new management, we can promise every Old Boy an excellent Dinner, and we hope to make this year a record success in every way. One thing we do ask,—MAY WE HAVE YOUR REPLY EARLY to facilitate Catering arrangements.

11 0 p.m.	Round the Lamp.

Sunday, November 28th

10 45 a.m.	SPECIAL SERVICE in the ILKLEY CONGREGATIONAL CHURCH.
	Golf on the Ilkley Club Links.

Accommodation for the Weekend may be booked on application to Troutbeck Hydro.

ROLL UP TO THE TWENTY-SIXTH ANNUAL DINNER !

in Leeds repelling an attack on his tram, until a baton charge cleared the street;" another tells of working with five hundred others in the docks and gaining entry through thousands of workers at the gate "in twenty closed-in furniture vans." There is even an intimation a couple of years later of the shadow that is to fall across Europe when one Old Boy reports seeing Mussolini in the Coliseum "addressing the 16,000 Milanese workers who had come to Rome to demonstrate their devotion to 'il Duce'."

There were also developments closer to home. In 1925 an additional games field was purchased alongside the existing one and a scheme was introduced for erecting a small pavilion on it. There were plans for hot water in the changing rooms of the main pavilion, while in 1927 pupils returned from holiday to find that electric lighting had been installed in the school building. There was another inspection in 1927. By this time there were fewer boarders, only thirty three. Nevertheless, and despite some concerns at the reduction in the numbers of younger pupils, the conclusion was optimistic:

> Since the last inspection the School has made steady progress and is now very creditable. The high reputation of the School will probably attract boarders more freely as the economic situation improves.

The programme for the 1927 production of 'A Christmas Carol'.

However, there was talk of a much greater change, one which would fundamentally alter the School's character. Although the question of a dual school had been raised as far back as 1905, by 1923 Alderman P.R.Jackson, Chairman of the West Riding Education Committee lamented publicly in his Speech Day address that though "the school in Ilkley is one of the best grammar schools in the West Riding, I am only sorry they have not as good a school for girls as they have for boys." The School might have hoped the matter would end with that pious sentiment, but it did not. The policy of the West Riding was for more dual schools. In 1925 five acres of land adjoining the Grammar School were purchased with a view to making provision for girls. This was the land to the west of the building, where the tennis courts were later laid out and

PROGRAMME
XMAS-1927

where, in the next century, an entire new block would be built. At the same time the Governors "were asked to consider the question of reorganising the School to admit girls," but they felt it their duty as Trustees of the Boys' Grammar School Foundation to preserve its character and identity. However the issue would not go away. By 1929 the Editor of the Old Olicanian was sounding alarm bells:

> It may not be widely known among Old Boys that for some time representations have been made to the County authorities that a girls' secondary school in Ilkley is an urgent necessity. The West Riding's educational policy has always seemed to us more than a little unsound; and in some quarters it is perceived that the County, having committed themselves to more or less providing the accommodation asked for, would wish to whittle their promise down to something more acceptable to their purse. Robert Browning showed the County authorities years ago, in "The Pied Piper of Hamelin", that official action of this kind is dangerous to the welfare of the rising generation. The proposal of the West Riding authorities seems to be to convert the existing Grammar School into a dual school, and we feel justified in lodging a protest. An excellent dual school exists at Otley, and means of transport between the two towns are very good and ever improving. No marriage of true minds is possible between the present School, proud of its traditions, and this product of a rigorous economy which, at the risk of being ungallant, we are compelled to describe as unlovely in the extreme.

There was no doubt that Mr Frazer and the Governors stood four-square with the Old Boys. One can only guess at the machinations which took place to try to forestall an outcome many thought would be disastrous. The Old Olicanian of July 1930 thought the tide might have turned: "We hear that the dual school question has at last been dropped – not before time." When he resigned in 1933 Mr Frazer quite clearly thought the day had been won for, in his final address as Headmaster at the Old Olicanians' Dinner, he proudly announced "quite definitely that the menace of a dual school has gone."

His headship still had three years to run when, in 1930, the School mourned the deaths of two of the people it held most dear. The first was that of Francis Humphris at the age of 92. He, more than anyone, embodied its recent history. Known affectionately as 'Honolulu Humphris' (he had the distinction in 1906 of being elected Chairman of Governors when in Hawaii and posting his letter of acceptance from Honolulu), he had been a governor since 1886, in the days when there had been a governing body but no building, he had spent five separate periods as Chairman and his is a name which appears regularly on documents over forty or more years. The other was more immediate and quite unexpected. Miss Wylde died at the age of fifty. She had been appointed by Mr Atkinson in 1906 and was a sympathetic teacher whose responsibilities included the Preparatory Department. As the much-loved Head of Black House she was revered by generations of pupils. There was an eloquent tribute from an Old Boy:

Miss Wylde, much-loved Head of Black House, who died in 1930.

> When it was announced that she was coming to teach, the boys in the middle classes imagined they were to be introduced to someone who would receive without suspicion the ancient tricks of the school-room. Miss Wylde disarmed them instantly, but not by pedagogic strategy. She exercised a personal authority of which she herself scarcely seemed aware, and it was entirely effective. It showed itself in a vigour of mind and of movement which was hard to resist both because of its force and its humour. At that time she was teaching history to one of the senior forms and astonished that form, and others no less, by arriving one morning with a small alarm clock, which she placed upon the desk to mark the time of the lessons. That was felt to be extraordinary. But very soon the School found that there was no more friendly figure, or remembering figure to be met, swinging along the corridors, than Miss Wylde, with the alarm clock hanging from a finger.

A more permanent memorial to her came in 1934, when the names of the houses were changed, Red becoming Atkinson, Yellow Swann, Blue Frazer and, of course, Black becoming Wylde.

Mr Frazer resigned in 1933. He had not been well but he moved to Harrogate and later to Epsom and enjoyed twenty years' retirement. His successor was William B. Hillis, Senior Classics Master at Leeds Grammar School. He was a cultured man, well-travelled, well-read and a painter of merit. His style was, as the Inspection Report of 1938 makes clear, in considerable contrast to that of Mr Frazer:

> The Head Master has replaced the strict discipline of his predecessor by one based more on public opinion than on punishment. There is no reason why one method should not

October 1933 - "Reflections on the Old School cap: Ilkley Grammar School boys considering the merits of their new striped cap and the old one."

be as effective as the other, though public opinion may take a little time to educate. The Inspectors saw no signs of relaxed discipline, and found the boys pleasant and friendly.

The school Mr Hillis took over was not without its problems. Foremost among them was the drop in numbers during the 1930s. When boarding had been abolished in 1932 numbers had actually risen slightly, perhaps due to the freeing up of the former dormitories for classrooms. But there was also the usual competition from neighbouring schools, most particularly from Prince Henry's in Otley, which had by now moved into a new building. The County Council suggested the Preparatory School be closed but the Governors resisted. Fees were reduced drastically, from £15 to £9 9s but numbers continued to decline.

The Olicanian acquired a supplement devoted to the arts, while continuing to chronicle events both local and national. The Great Flood of February 1935, is dramatically described by A.S. Jeffrey:

I went down at 9 o'clock to the New Bridge, and already the river was out at many places; I went down several times during the morning and each time the river had risen with great rapidity. All along the north side of the New Bridge it had converted the low lying ground into a series of lakes. The natural course of the river could not be distinguished; many trees were torn up by the roots and were being swept down the river. Although it was so wet there were a great many people going down to look at it. Some enterprising coal merchant lent one of his vans to take people across the flooded road at the bottom of New Brook Street. Many people were wading across, but later in the afternoon the water became too deep. One of the saddest things was the number of animals that were drowned. After lunch a friend took me down to Ben Rhydding Toll Bridge, about 2 o'clock; the river was still rising very fast and the wind was still very fierce. It was flowing two feet over the bridge, which shook violently when the thundering water struck it, and the trees coming down damaged the bridge on the west side. On Monday morning I went to look at what was left of Addingham Swing Bridge, which had been completely torn up and washed away.

In the same year King George V and Queen Mary celebrated their Silver Jubilee. R.Storey writes of the fire on Beamsley Beacon and of how he decorated his bike:

I, like most people, arose early and decorated my bicycle with red, white and blue paper. I made a shield of cardboard, painted it silver, pasting on photos of our King and Queen; between these I put G.M.R., and underneath a home-made Union Jack. When I had finished decorating my bicycle I decorated the house front.

You can sense the grief of D.J.M. when, a year later, the King dies: "Our King was dead, our great little King, a soldier, a sailor, a sportsman, he who loved his country so much, and whose voice we had heard broadcasted all over the world at Christmas." The Coronation in 1937 and the visit of the new King George VI and Queen Elizabeth to Otley, when two motor buses were hired to convey pupils, are also commemorated. But there are darker strains. As early as 1935 the use to which the swastika is being put elsewhere causes concern:

Being, as is well known, the original owners of the Swastika, we naturally take a proprietor's interest in its present turbulent course on the continent. We hope that the present exhibition of flag-waving may not culminate in an even more devastating orgy of bloodshed than that through which our predecessors went in 1914-18.

William Hillis, Headmaster from 1933 to 1942.

School First XV 1934 - 35.

Back Row: R. Heel, G. Weightman, Stokes, Green, Plummer, N. Butler, Burnell.
Middle Row: P. Brumfitt, K. Haigh, J. Brumfitt, N.Whitaker, S. Walbank.
Front Row: J. Naylor, V. Bassett.

In early 1938, with the invasion of Austria and Czechoslovakia, there is a defiant jauntiness:

> In spite of almost weekly crises in Europe, we do not, as yet, come to school in gas masks, nor have we constructed dug-outs in the field. In fact this last term has been quite normal at school except for the converting of the old dormitories to classrooms, and a visit from some Shakespearean players.

By 1939 events have moved on:

> This term – as well as last – there has been great excitement over world affairs caused of course by Hitler and his activities. This, to a certain extent, has even spread to School, though, among the Lower School at least, it has been centred chiefly in the distribution of gas masks. In the Upper School there has been a great deal of argument, and incidentally disagreement, on the subject of Mr Chamberlain.

Mindful of the growing threat, the Governors agreed in February 1939 "to allow the School for use in an emergency for the collection of children prior to their re-distribution to billets." At the same time the County Education Officer stated that "it is intended that, in the event of a National Emergency involving evacuation of children, it is deemed desirable to billet 300 Secondary School pupils from Leeds Modern School in the area of Ilkley Grammar School." In response to appalling events already unfolding elsewhere, a governor asked "whether, in case a number of non-Aryan refugee children from Central Europe about 11 years of age should be received in Ilkley, it would be possible to offer them an education at the Grammar School, and whether the Governors would be able to reduce the fee."

Amid growing fears of another major European convulsion, life continued with the appearance of normality. Under the influence of Mr Hillis the magazine took on a more literary flavour; indeed he gave a talk to the Literary Society on Modern Poetry, including observations on Hopkins, Hardy, MacNeice and Eliot. There was a major Art Exhibition with the outstanding feature a frieze "some 30 feet long, illustrating 'Country Life' with poachers, shooting, shire horses and all those things to be found in the country." Governors, faced with an ailing mower, decided "to discard the 33-inch Ransome horse machine and the car which draws it and to purchase a 36-inch motor mower, which could be housed in the Nissen hut." The traditions of Speech Day, Empire Day and Armistice Day were still observed: "On Armistice Day [1938] poppies were sold in the school and at eleven o'clock we all assembled in Big School for the Silence and to hear the broadcast of the service from the Cenotaph. The sale of poppies raised £1 9s." Tributes were paid to John W. Dixon, Clerk to the Governors for thirty five years, who died at the end of 1938. The achievement in the same year of former pupil Jack Brumfitt in being selected for the Yorkshire cricket team was celebrated. His captain that day, and indeed the county captain from 1933 until 1947, was A.B. (Brian) Sellers, also a former pupil, albeit as a boarder in the Preparatory School. Meanwhile the President of the Old Olicanians for 1938-39 was W.M. (Billy) Dalton, a "Swann Boy," whose investiture brought to light the following story:

> In the "Swann Days" the number of scholars was less than a hundred. Mr Atkinson announced one morning that the total had reached ninety-nine and promised a half holiday when the hundredth was enrolled. Billy rolled up in the afternoon with "our Percy" and claimed the half holiday. Some time later the Head met Mr Dalton senior at his club and informed him that there were now one hundred and ninety-nine boys in the school. "Could he do anything about it?" Mr Dalton replied that he would send "our Jim," but that he could not make any promises if the school roll should increase to two hundred and ninety-nine!

But behind the facade of normality, the old question of the dual school had re-surfaced. The main problem was numbers. They had declined from 211 in 1935 to 163 in 1938, while it was deemed the building had accommodation for 278. At the same time the schools at Otley and Aireborough were full, so much so that they were requesting building extensions. The catch was that they were full because they took the girls from Ilkley – no fewer than 104 at Otley and a further 14 at Aireborough. Given that the schools were so close to each other, it made sense to consider the issue as a whole. Two possible solutions were identified. The first was that Otley would remain mixed, Ilkley would remain all-boys and Aireborough would become all-girls. However there could be no guarantee that all the Ilkley girls would go to Aireborough, any more than that boys from the farther reaches of the Aireborough catchment, such as Horsforth, would make the daily journey to Ilkley in preference to some of the closer Leeds schools. The alternative, as outlined in the relevant minute, was "to revive the suggestion which has previously been discussed with the Governors and to make Ilkley into a Mixed School serving its own area." It was a proposal which made sense; each school would serve its local community rather than the girls from Ilkey and the boys from Aireborough passing each other in opposite directions every day. The clinching argument, as in all such matters, was financial. It made little sense to spend money on extensions at Otley and Aireborough while there was surplus capacity at Ilkley. The Governors could not defy the West Riding for ever. The School received a grant of £5,000 a year from the County without which it could not continue. In the end there could be no debate.

On 8th November 1938 the Governors wrote to the West Riding confirming that they had approved the change. The County was enthusiastic but had to consult those schools which would lose pupils in the process, "informing them of the suggested admission of girls to Ilkley Grammar School and giving them the opportunity of expressing their views on the proposals." There was some disagreement over parental choice for those pupils in Menston and Burley gaining County Minor Scholarships, which was resolved by allowing Menston parents a free choice between the three schools, while those from Burley, which was within the Urban District, were initially allocated to Ilkley, though parents could subsequently opt for Otley or Aireborough. Then there was the question of accommodation. Even though the additional five acres had been bought in 1925 specifically for girls, no one was suggesting expansion. Modification was all that could be afforded: "The Education Architect is being asked to report on the possibility of utilising the present premises at Ilkley for boys and girls, and the alterations which would be necessary to complete the change from a Boys' to a Mixed School." All that resulted was some piecemeal adaptation costing £660. In March 1939 the Board of Education approved the change and a historic amendment was made to the Scheme for the Governance of the School:

> The School of the Foundation shall be a Day School and, if the Governors see fit, a Boarding School, for boys and girls, and shall be maintained in or near the Parish of Ilkley, in the present school buildings or in other suitable buildings provided by the Governors, as a Public Secondary School. The term 'Boys' hereinafter referred to in the Scheme shall also include Girls.

There were the inevitable protests from the Old Olicanian:

> If the suggested change should materialise, the whole character of the School would be changed, in our opinion for the worse. Old Boys would generally lose all interest in the School, and this in turn would have a detrimental effect on its future.

The Governors fended off the last remnants of pressure, noting at their meeting on 3rd January 1939 the receipt of "a letter from the

Old Boys' Olicanian Association (which had already appeared in the press) protesting against the scheme to take girl pupils at the School. The Headmaster was asked to write . . . assuring the Old Boys' Association that the matter had been fully considered by Governors before making a decision."

By and large, the inevitability of change came to be accepted. The tone of the Olicanian for Summer 1939 was welcoming, if patronising:

> We look forward with interest and expectation to the coming of girls. We are glad to hear that there are a great many applications already and hope that they will soon settle down into our ways. Perhaps next year one of them will be writing this editorial! We shall welcome their assistance in this and many other departments of school life.

On Sunday 3rd September 1939 Britain declared war on Germany. On Tuesday 12th September ninety girls were admitted to Ilkley Grammar School, joining classes throughout the School. Things would never be quite the same again.

At War Again

After two decades of stability, the changes came thick and fast. The most immediate wartime danger was thought to be from air raids and no time was lost in making the building as secure as possible. Stirrup pumps and sand were bought and the windows were treated with anti-splinter liquid coating, but the Education Authority "declined to authorise expenditure on the strengthening of the basement of the school for air raid precautions." Although there were bombing raids on Leeds and Bradford, the nearest Ilkley came to being attacked was when a bomb was dropped on Bolton Abbey cricket field and another demolished a wall at Beamsley. The promised evacuation began, with children from more vulnerable industrial centres being moved to the relative safety of rural areas. Leeds Modern School duly arrived as guests of the Grammar School. The Headmaster, Dr Morton, lived in a flat attached to the Headmaster's house. As well as 90 extra girls, the building now had to accommodate a further 277 evacuees. The only solution was to alternate teaching, so the Leeds children used it in the morning and Ilkley children in the afternoon. This arrangement continued until 1941, when the Leeds pupils returned home. The 'black-out' and the inevitable transport restrictions limited school activities. The Education Authority recommended fewer governors' meetings "with a view to avoidance of unnecessary travelling and the multiplication of demands on public men in the present emergency." Paper was scarce and the Olicanian was not produced from 1941 to 1944. In the last issue before it was suspended, two of the new girls, Joan Verity and Barbara Sparham, caught the mood:

> On the Friday before the war, Ilkley was as busy as any town. The reason is that Ilkley is in the safety area and some of the children from Leeds were being evacuated here. Buses and trains all that day and the day after were bringing in children from Leeds. There is now a 'Communal Feeding Centre' for the evacuees, thus relieving householders of the children at lunchtime. The black-out has affected everyone. On 2nd September every householder was ordered to black out the windows so that not a chink of light should be seen from outside. For the first few weeks of the war people were

warned by the police or the air raid warden to attend to their lights. Later on, an order was issued that if anyone had a light showing they would be fined. In December rationing was brought into force. The goods rationed are butter, bacon, sugar and meat. Most people are managing on their rations. Rationing, I suppose, is essential during war-time, but, for people such as me, it will become most trying, for I have such an enormous appetite. I suppose, though, that I ought not to grumble, because the German people are a great deal worse off than we are.

For the evacuees, Ilkley turned out not to be quite what they had expected. One wrote:

One always imagines that an evacuation town is a little inactive place with no connections with civilisation, with one general store and with a few scattered cottages, and even the impression gained by letter was deceiving. These ideas were entirely frustrated when I arrived and I was delighted to find that the town even boasted a Woolworth's.

And another:

I arrived in Ilkley fully expecting to see a desolate village surrounded by bleak moorland, but instead I saw a little town in a sheltered valley and people walking about the streets wearing modern clothes.

Even around Ilkley there could be danger. Derek Hyatt recalls finding what he thought was a dummy hand grenade on Langbar Moor:

It looked like one that my father had used in the Home Guard. In fact, it was a live grenade, the pin had been pulled out and the only reason it did not explode was that it was caked in mud. I cycled all the way back down from Langbar Moor with the grenade bouncing about in the basket in the front of my bike. When I got back to Ilkley I was stopped by the local Home Guard who asked me what I had in my basket. When he saw the grenade he said, "Just prop your bike against that lamp-post and we'll call the bomb disposal unit." At morning assembly the next day the Headmaster explained that someone had brought "something dangerous" into town the previous evening and asked that anyone who had any such souvenirs bring them into school the following day without fear of reprisal. When we got to school the next morning, the entrance looked like an armoury!

The School had changed dramatically with the advent of girls, though the outbreak of war made it one change among many. Numbers had increased to almost 300. There were now ten women on the staff and the first female governors were appointed. Mr Hillis welcomed the new pupils: "I think I may say without fear of exaggerating that the present party of girls, both in their separate activities and in what they contribute to the common life of the school as a whole, have made a very definite success of their first two terms and leave us with no further doubts on the wisdom of accepting them." Domestic Science was added to the curriculum and taught in a wooden hut erected on the field; hockey and netball were added to the games played and there were school team reports for them alongside those for rugby and cricket. But there were no proper facilities for the new sports. Hockey was played at various times on West Holmes Field, at Ben Rhydding

September 1939 - and girls arrive at Ilkley Grammar School for the first time.

Sports Club, at Ilkley cricket ground and on one of the Valley Drive playing fields. Netball was played on the Craiglands tennis courts. Even classroom accommodation was barely adequate. And yet everybody seemed to be enjoying themselves. "We laughed a lot at Ilkley Grammar School in those days," wrote one of the new girls. "There hadn't been much laughter at my previous school. Laughter wasn't ladylike." The Editor of the Olicanian (presumably a boy) was in no doubt that things had improved:

> The girls have added new life and vigour to the various societies of the School, and have assisted in the resurrection of the Literary Society. A joint class for Ballroom Dancing was started this term, and it is hoped that as a result of this extra educational facility made possible by the coming of the girls, most of the seniors leaving the School this coming summer will have a fair knowledge of Dancing, though we hope they will not become "demented jitterbugs."

Yet behind all this novelty there was a war going on. By 1941 there were long lists of "Old Boys Serving in H.M. Forces" and, in a depressing echo of events twenty five years earlier, the first names of deaths began to appear in the Olicanian, until it was suspended in 1941, and in the pages of the Ilkley Gazette. There was John King who had been Assistant Scoutmaster of the School Troop, Dennis Smith, aged only nineteen, a dispatch rider with the Royal Corps of Signals, Colin Murray, who had been sports champion in 1939, Basil Greaves also nineteen, who had gone straight into the army from school, James McCormack, who died in a prisoner of war camp in Burma; the waste of young lives goes on being reported. There is more hopeful news of those who have been captured. One of them, John Normanton, imprisoned near Dresden, wrote poetry, later published as "Frail Prelude." The opening of one piece catches the frustration and yearnings of a prisoner:

> *My tears have flowed inward many a year,*
> *Drenching in bitterness my tired heart*
> *With sour salt of sorrow, taste of fear.*

Unlike the First War, when virtually all the deaths had been in France, this was truly a World War, with fatalities reported from the skies over England, the fields of Europe, the deserts of North Africa and the jungles of the Far East.

As before, the School did its bit. An Air Training Corps was formed. Though not strictly a school organisation, it met on school premises and many of its members were pupils. Ilkley's

Special Constables were allowed the use of the gymnasium one evening per week at the nominal charge of 4/6d. The acreage of the school garden was doubled. Boys went off to pick potatoes at 6d. an hour and helped with the harvest and haymaking at local farms. A Savings Group was established, and, during the Ilkley War Weapons Week, excelled itself by purchasing over a thousand certificates. Although the School argued successfully for the retention of its iron railings, those round the two Valley Drive playing fields were commandeered "for salvage."

In the middle of all this activity, and in an uncanny echo of events during the First War, the Headmaster died. Mr Hillis had been ill for eighteen months, during which time much of the detailed organisation had been in the capable hands of Mr Evans, the Senior Master. Nevertheless Mr Hillis' death in August 1942 came as a shock, for only a month earlier, following an operation, it had been reported that he expected soon to be back at work.

The First XV Rugby Team 1939 - 40.

Left to Right: Back Row: W. Hardwick, D. Keighley, W. Henderson, J. Atkinson, T. Wheatcroft, B. Armitage, G. Hodges, R. Ellwood, G. Castle (Secretary).
Front Row: J. Marland, J. Holmes, R. Morgan, J. Segrott, J.Sinclair, J. Ingham, F. Moon.

Some governors had been so impressed with Mr Evans as Acting Head that they wanted to appoint him without the post being advertised, but the West Riding insisted on correct procedures. In November 1942 John S. Newby, Headmaster of Whitcliffe Mount School, Cleckheaton was appointed and took up the post in May 1943. There were other breaks with the past. In February 1943 Mr Lovelock collapsed and died in the staffroom one morning just before assembly; he had been on the staff since 1918. Mr Frazer, who had known him as a boy at Whitgift School, Croydon wrote, "No one but myself could appreciate the unsparing hard work and the loyal help which made him a perfect colleague." The following year an even older link was severed with the death of Mr Eames, who had been a master since 1909. There was genuine warmth in the tributes. An Old Boy serving in India wrote:

> He was a grand man, and a very good friend to all who knew him. If he could give anyone a helping hand, nothing was too much trouble for him, and we always had a cheery smile and a pleasant word whenever he was about. There will never be another 'Old Eamo'.

H.W.Brumfitt, an Old Boy and Governor, paid tribute in the Gazette:

> Mr Eames was the last remaining link with the days when Mr C.W. Atkinson was Headmaster. Mr Atkinson's motto was "Fear God, Honour the King and be gentlemen." Mr Eames always tried to carry that out, and not only tried but was eminently successful.

John Newby, Headmaster from 1943 to 1954.

It cannot have been easy for Mr Newby to gather up the threads of a school beset by so many changes in such a short time. Ironically, all the surplus accommodation evident in 1938 was now being fully utilised and was proving insufficient. In his first Speech Day address in 1943, celebrating the fiftieth year of the School's revival, Mr Newby deplored the overcrowding and hoped, rather optimistically, for some new building work once the war was over. It was not to be. Apart from the Domestic Science hut, one other Nissen hut was constructed for the ATC, later becoming the dining room, and that was about it. Throughout the war – and for some time afterwards – lunches were served in the WVS canteen – itself a converted garage – on Leeds Road and pupils trooped to and fro in all weathers.

Mr. Newby saw the importance of "reviving the School Magazine in the middle of our national struggle for existence" though it could only re-appear as a leaflet. He tried to ensure that, even in trying times, school life was as rich as possible. He understood the importance of parental involvement and started a Parents' Association "to foster a sense of corporate spirit" and, inevitably, "to explore opportunities of extending the equipment and amenities of the School." Societies continued to flourish. The house system was again overhauled, mainly because of the difficulty of raising teams from insufficient numbers. They were reduced to three and re-named, with a classical flourish, Athens, Sparta and Troy. Efforts continued "to help people whose part in the war is more active than our own." Through sales, collections and entertainments, £49 13s. 5d. was raised and donated to such causes as the Merchant Navy Comforts' Fund, the Red Cross, the Prisoners of War Fund and the purchase of cigarettes for the Eighth Army. A War Savings Group was established in 1940 and within four years had raised over £5,700. Some forms made "bibs and frocks for bombed-out babies." Vitya Babayev, a Russian boy from Orel and living in the Pravda Home near Moscow, was adopted by some of the juniors, who wrote to him and sent him gifts. Pupils assisted the national effort to collect rose-hips for

The Second World War Memorial in the School Library

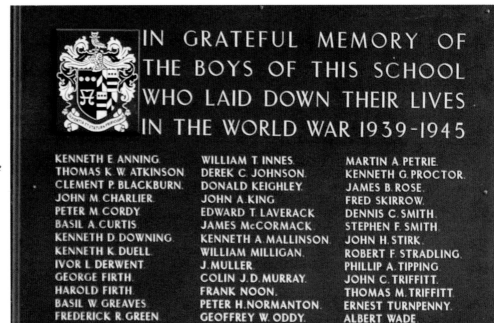

IN GRATEFUL MEMORY OF THE BOYS OF THIS SCHOOL WHO LAID DOWN THEIR LIVES IN THE WORLD WAR 1939-1945

KENNETH E ANNING.
THOMAS K. W. ATKINSON.
CLEMENT P. BLACKBURN.
JOHN M. CHARLIER.
PETER M. CORDY.
BASIL A. CURTIS.
KENNETH D. DOWNING.
KENNETH K. DUELL.
IVOR L. DERWENT.
GEORGE FIRTH.
HAROLD FIRTH.
BASIL W. GREAVES.
FREDERICK R. GREEN.
ARTHUR HILTON.

WILLIAM T. INNES.
DEREK C. JOHNSON.
DONALD KEIGHLEY.
JOHN A. KING.
EDWARD T. LAVERACK.
JAMES McCORMACK.
KENNETH A. MALLINSON.
WILLIAM MILLIGAN.
J. MULLER.
COLIN J. D. MURRAY.
FRANK NOON.
PETER H. NORMANTON.
GEOFFREY W. ODDY.
FRED PEACE.

MARTIN A. PETRIE.
KENNETH G. PROCTOR.
JAMES B. ROSE.
FRED SKIRROW.
DENNIS C. SMITH.
STEPHEN F. SMITH.
JOHN H. STIRK.
ROBERT F. STRADLING.
PHILLIP A. TIPPING.
JOHN C. TRIFFITT.
THOMAS M. TRIFFITT.
ERNEST TURNPENNY.
ALBERT WADE.
DEREK WALKER.

JAMES D. WILLOUGHBY.   JOHN H. WIRE.

Vitamin C Syrup. A group of girls went off to Cambridgeshire to help with the fruit-picking. Many boys worked on farms during the holidays and, to his credit, Mr Newby managed to visit every one. The boys enjoyed the work and especially being "paid reg'lar."

Meanwhile discussions about the organisation of schools were taking place in Parliament. These culminated in the 1944 Butler Education Act which had far-reaching consequences throughout the country. Henceforth the old elementary schools would disappear and would be replaced by primary and secondary with the age of transfer fixed at 11. There would be an examination, the 11-plus, which would be taken by children in their final year at primary school and which would determine which of three types of secondary school, grammar, technical or modern, they would attend. There was provision for comprehensive or multi-lateral schools, which combined all three, as well as direct grant schools which were independent of local authority control and were funded by a grant directly from the Ministry of Education.

The fact that so many changes were taking place between 1939 and 1945 has the effect, from a historical perspective, of drawing attention away from the nightmare of the war. The Second World War was fought on more fronts than the 1914-18 conflict and hence, despite the vast death toll and manifest atrocities, it seemed at times to lack the concentrated immediacy and horror of trench warfare and the stalemate of the Western Front. Perhaps partly because the school magazine ceased production for three years and the Old Olicanians suspended all activities, it is simply not as well documented. There seem to be fewer letters home or to the School, none of the regular termly lists of casualties focused relentlessly in the Olicanian, less of the patriotic fervour. Yet if we should seek proof of the courage and heroism of a second generation of Olicanians we should look no further than the commemorative plaque on the library wall, where, alongside the Great War deaths, are added a further forty four names. Once again, there was joy when the war was over but it was accompanied by the sobering knowledge that it had been a victory dearly bought.

A Changing World

For the second time in a little over a quarter of a century there was a victory to be celebrated. There were cheers and smiles when Mr Newby announced Admiral Doenitz's surrender on May 7th 1945. The school flag was hauled up to the accompaniment of cheers for each of the Army, Navy and Air Force. Molly Shaw described it all:

> Breaking the flag on the afternoon of VE Day caused a great sensation. During the last lesson of the day Mr. Newby came to tell each form to march quietly outside to see the new flag broken. He seemed rather disappointed because VE Day had not been announced while we were at school. The wireless had been kept going in the School Hall in anticipation of the expected announcement and the School had managed to secure a new flagstaff and Union Jack. He explained that, though the official VE announcement would not be given until later in the evening, it was now definite that all German armies had surrendered unconditionally, and we were entitled to celebrate that. Once the school was outside, the breaking of the flag ceremony took but a few minutes. The Caretaker, assisted, or probably hindered, by a few boys, hauled up the new flag, amidst cheers and laughter from the whole school, including the staff. Everyone was pleased to see how beautifully the flag floated along in the breeze.

Sixth formers helped to build a bonfire at the rugby field and crowds flocked to see it lit at ten o'clock by repatriated prisoners of war. The following day all the Ilkley schools joined in a Thanksgiving Service at St Margaret's Church. In the evening a School Victory Ball was held in the Hall; music was provided by a radiogram borrowed from the local youth club, there was community singing in the interval and ice cream was served. To cap it all, a two-day holiday was granted, all the more welcome for being added to the school closure for polling day.

Amidst all the joy, there was sadness that so many had not returned. Fourteen-year-old P. Mellor of Athens House wrote a moving tribute which began:

Now that the war is over in Europe, let us not forget those who gave their lives that we might live in peace. Let us reverence them and, although they are dead, let us see to it that their spirit lives on for ever.

Within a month of VE Day the new sense of European unity was given tangible form, with the establishing of a "compact of friendship" with the Lycée de Coutances, a French grammar school on the coast of Normandy. As early as 1932 M. Blériot from the Lycée had visited the West Riding when an elaborate scheme of exchange and friendship between schools in the vicinity of Leeds University and those in the area of the University of Lille had been inaugurated. With the end of the war and through the services of a mutual friend, the two Headmasters were able to renew contact. Very soon lists of pupils were being drawn up and before long letters were crossing the Channel in both directions. It was intended that exchange visits should begin as soon as possible but there were problems at the French end; the town had been badly bombed during the Allied invasion in June 1944 and many of the school buildings had been damaged or destroyed. Indeed it was not until July 24th 1947 that the first exchange took place, with sixteen French pupils arriving in Ilkley. Even then there were a few problems. The majority of English who wished to go to France were girls, while the majority of French who wanted to come to England were boys. This was presumably settled to everyone's satisfaction. Then it was discovered that holders of collective passports were denied foreign currency and it took the fortuitous intervention of a Military Field Officer at Southampton, Keith Dixon, who just happened to be an Old Olicanian, to ensure a smooth passage through customs, a welcome breakfast and envelopes containing some English small change. From these modest beginnings, due largely to the efforts of Bob Swallow and Georges Lechaptois, there grew the annual exchange visits which continue to this day. They have given thousands of young people an opportunity to live with an English or French family, in some cases to establish life-long friendships and in at least one case to celebrate an Anglo-French marriage. From the school pairing have grown similar arrangements, civic, musical, sporting and many others, culminating in the formal twinning of the two towns. It is a happy chance that the sixtieth anniversary of the exchange should have coincided with the four hundredth anniversary of the School.

Gradually the rhythms of peacetime life were resumed. In November 1945 the 51st Speech Day was held in the King's Hall. The guests were the newly-elected M.P. for Pudsey and Otley, Col. Malcolm Stoddart-Scott and his wife. The school play was

"Toad of Toad Hall." There was the usual round of games fixtures. Societies covered such disparate areas as Drama, Current Affairs and Debating, Science, Music and Gramophone, Geography and Naturalists. The Scout Troop was re-started by Norman Salmon in 1947. In the same year the old ATC hut was adapted to replace the inadequate dining accommodation. There were visits to Malvern Wells, the Lake District, North Wales and the Yorkshire Dales. While the distances involved may seem modest, we should not underestimate the transport problems of those days. As Myra Hopkinson reported, even a visit to Gordale Scar could induce anxiety:

End of term assembly 1945 - on the front lawn. Mr Newby addresses the School.

How the bus managed to get there is something of a mystery, as the driver was seen to be struggling furiously, and folding his hands in prayer on some of the steeper hills. Some hills had to be attempted twice; some had to be walked up, the bus sheepishly following amid groans and clanks.

The agricultural camps continued beyond the end of the war in Europe, the boys in the East Riding and the girls in Chipping Campden returning home the day before VJ Day was declared. The link with the High School in Missoula, Montana, begun during the war, continued; distance prevented any exchange but there was a constant flow of letters and information. In October 1945 the Old Olicanians' Association resumed activities. It was still strictly a male preserve, the Old Girls' Association, formed in 1943, enjoying a parallel but separate existence. In 1946, in a gesture to mark the conclusion of the first seven-year course for girls, Mrs Kingswell, Headmistress of Wakefield Girls' High School, became the first woman to be the principal guest at Speech Day. The Parents' Association was, as ever, raising money to help supplement school equipment; fresh from having purchased an episcope, they were now saving hard for a cine projector. Times were hard. It was even necessary to take a collection at Sports Day, the Headmaster reminding spectators that the West Riding allowance for sports equipment was still the same as it had been in 1939.

Mr Newby and staff shortly after the war.

Meanwhile the School was coming to terms with the implications of the 1944 Act. The policy of the West Riding was to plan for the introduction of comprehensive schools and its initial proposal for Ilkley was "that when a site is purchased for the erection of a new Modern School, such site be sufficiently large for a multi-lateral school to be built on it." The Governors wanted to explore the possibilities of direct grant status and the Chairman, Mr Findlay, and the Headmaster were dispatched to Wakefield to float the idea with the Chief Education Officer, Mr Clegg. They soon got their answer. The County Education Committee passed a resolution that "the Governors of Ripon and Ilkley Grammar Schools be informed that any application of either Board of Governors to the Ministry of Education for direct grant status would be opposed at every stage." The Governors responded by undertaking "to give the most careful consideration to any proposal for a new comprehensive school on an appropriate site," knowing full well that in the prevailing conditions of post-war austerity any major building programme would be out of the question. Instead, in 1946, they came up with another idea. With only a few extra rooms the School might move to a three form entry "for Grammar and Technical courses." The idea was never taken up and was only one of several proposals in protracted negotiations which went on for years. One senses something of a ritual dance about it all. The Authority knew what it wanted but couldn't afford it. The School knew what it wanted but had to play for time.

The West Riding was required to provide the Ministry of Education with a Development Plan and by March 1947 Mr Clegg had submitted the latest version with the comment, "I am instructed to inform you that the Authority do not approve the suggestion that Ilkley Grammar School should continue as a Unilateral Grammar School." As late as September 1949 it was stated at a Governors' meeting that "the County Education Committee's preference is for a Multi-lateral School for Ilkley." In the end the Governors' strategy of holding out, allied to the sheer impossibility of the County's plans being realised, forced the issue. The Development Plan could not be held up for ever and on 14th February 1950 Mr Clegg conceded:

> The Education Committee have now considered the views of your Governors . . . on the revised Development Plan for secondary education. The Committee resolved that the Plan be amended to provide for the retention of the school as a 2 form entry Secondary (Grammar) School, and that the Secondary Technical provision for the area for both boys and girls be centralised at Otley.

The School's status was established as a Voluntary (Controlled) Secondary School, which meant that the County was to be responsible for the maintenance of buildings, and that the teachers, though appointed by the Governors, were to be in the service of the County. There was some debate over who should be responsible for the Headmaster's house, with the County eventually accepting both the responsibility and the rents. Henceforth two thirds of the Governors were appointed by the County while a third were Governors of the Foundation. A small, separate group of Foundation Governors remained to disburse leaving scholarships and the relatively small sums accruing from earlier investments. Further consequences of the Act were the closure of the Preparatory Department in 1947 and the abolition of fees. Secondary provision in the area was to be completed by the provision of a four-form entry Secondary (Modern) School.

Prizes were presented at the 1947 Speech Day by the Chairman of Governors, George Dean. Sadly, it was to be one of his last acts on behalf of the School for he died only a few weeks later.

This photograph was captioned: "Ilkley Grammar School girls in training for Sports Day 1947." The fact that several are wearing blazers suggests this may have been a photo shoot rather than a rigorous preparation.

Sports Day 1947 - the judges' table.

Left to Right: Miss Jackson, Miss Brown, Mr Bartle, Miss Skeel, Mr Swallow, Miss Worthington.

Sports Day 1947: Whittaker beats Melville to the tape. Mr Swallow and Mr Evans judge the finish.

His had been a long association. His father had been head of the firm that had built the present school. He and other members of his family attended, starting in 1894. His sister married one of the masters, his sons were pupils and he was President of the Old Olicanians in the mid-thirties. He was keenly involved in a variety of local affairs and was a great supporter of the School and its activities.

For many pupils school life was a rich experience. There were talented teachers on the staff and the School had not only coped with, but drawn strength from, the many recent changes. However there could also be a less pleasant side, as Tony Barringer recalls:

Off to camp! The Scout Troop on the front drive in the 1940s.

> For the boys, sanitation consisted of a great millstone-grit edifice at the bottom of the playground; profoundly unhygienic, open to the elements, approached by a terrifyingly steep flight of stairs with wrought iron railings. Part of the initiation ceremony for new boys was to be thrust in droves down into that dreadful place. It was known as 'The Bastille'. There was an undertone of physical violence which was, at times, frightening. Bullying was common and fights frequent, some of them well-publicised and seldom stopped by staff. Classic confrontations between senior boys and staff became part of legend. Certain prefects had a sadistic streak and one of the worst experiences was to be lashed with lengths of rubber tubing in labs by science-sixth

prefects. Anecdotes abounded of senior girls knocked unconscious for talking and of boys breaking out of class to be pursued by a rugby-playing teacher who vaulted down the staircase in an effort to catch the terrified boy. The most horrendous episode was a beating inflicted with cricket stumps on a member of the rugby team for some minor indiscretion.

The curriculum was not untypical of grammar schools throughout the country. It was relatively narrow and focused on matriculation, leading to university entrance. Options were restricting, with the Arts/Science divide occurring as early as the age of twelve. Practical subjects were not taken particularly seriously and streaming was rigid. The difference between 4A and 4B was, as Derek Hyatt recalled, absolute:

I was suddenly moved from 4A to 4B – an administrative requirement so that each class had equal numbers. All my friends were in 4A. 4B was notorious. 4B was a madhouse. 4A were all bound for university. 4B were all doomed. I exaggerate only slightly.

Meanwhile the final act in the drama of the dual school debate was being played out. When, with the return of those who had been on active service, the all-male Old Olicanians' Association was resurrected in 1945, the Old Girls' Association had already been in existence for two years. Mr. Newby favoured amalgamation. In November 1946 consideration was given at an Old Boys' Dinner to a draft constitution for a joint body which had already been agreed by the Girls' Association. After a "tedious discussion" the matter was referred back to the committee for revision. By May 1947 a Joint Committee had been formed to iron out problems, the main one of which seemed to be the position of the Head, who was President of one Association but not of the other. The eventual solution was that the Head would be on the committee but not as President. Thus it was that at the fortieth Old Boys' Dinner on 8th November 1947 it was agreed that a joint "Old Olicanians' Association" should henceforth exist. It is indicative of the strong sense of tradition, allied to a lingering unwillingness in some quarters to accept the mixed school, that such a minor matter should have dragged on for so long. Even within the new Association there were still separate functions. The first Old Girls' Dinner was held in 1952 at the Troutbeck Hotel. It was not until 1959, a full twenty years after girls had joined the School, that the first joint Dinner Dance was held.

The School Hockey Team 1948/49.

Back row l to r:
V. Outterside, K. Bubb,
T.T. Ranter,
J. Threlfall,
B. Dixon,
E. Petty.

Front row l to r:
D. Myers,
N. Town,
B. Miller,
S. Wright,
A. Law.

The School Rugby First XV 1948/49 with Mr Newby and Mr Walker.

Back row l to r:
P.J. Hirst,
M. Goldsborough,
S. Ackroyd,
B. Dakin,
J.W. Boocock,
A.W. Smith,
A. Chapman,
J. Williamson,
B. Simmons.

Front row l to r:
K. Plunkett,
B. Lupton,
B. Bingham,
H. Melville,
E. Potts,
J. Tonner,
A. Smith.

The School provided child singers for Covent Garden operas in Leeds. Here, in April 1949, a group rehearses with Music teacher Charles Bainbridge.

Prefects 1948 - 1949.

Back Row. l to r: E. Clark, V. Outterside, J. Ritchie, T.T. Ranter, A. Chapman, N. Manners, Litten, B. Bingham,
Front Row l to r: K. Bubb, M. Shaw, Miss Brown, Mr Newby, Mr Evans, D.H. Clarke, J.W. Boocock.

In 1950 the secondary plan for Ilkley under the 1944 Act was finally agreed. Prior to this, children not attending the Grammar School from the age of eleven completed the entirety of their education at one of the local elementary schools from the ages of 5-14, and 5-15 when the school leaving age was raised in 1947. Once the decision had been made to reorganise, events moved with unaccustomed speed. On 24th April 1950 Ben Rhydding Council School became Ilkley Ben Rhydding County School, with junior and senior sections and with Dan Jennings as Headmaster. He was succeeded a year later by Henry Brabban. The school accommodated those children who did not pass the new eleven-plus exam. The log book for the first day records:

> The number on roll this morning is 199 (Seniors). Furniture and books from the contributory schools have come with the senior children from Ilkley National School (Boys' Dept. and Girls' Dept.), Burley National School (Mixed), Burley Main St. Council School (Mixed) and Burley Woodhead (Mixed).

However, as Mary Weatherall, who was on the staff on that first day and later taught at the Grammar School, recalls, the school was not large enough to accommodate the entire intake:

> As it couldn't take such a large influx, the children were housed in Ben Rhydding Methodist Hall, Ilkley Congregational Church (now Christchurch) and One Oak, a large house in Wells Walk later taken over for a Nursery Nurses' Hostel. This was a horrendous period for both teachers and pupils. All the Ben Rhydding infants had to attend Ashlands or All Saints.

For the Grammar School the post-war years were a time of consolidation but they were not entirely free of change. In 1951 the School Certificate was succeeded by the General Certificate of Education. This meant that the old group or block certificate was replaced by the accumulation of passes in individual subjects. The view at the time was that this would affect the relative importance of subjects and lead to increased and earlier specialisation. The evidence suggests it was one of those changes which caused few problems and was quickly absorbed. The School was also caught up in the post-war enthusiasm for establishing international contacts. It joined the Council of Education in World Citizenship, sent parcels of food to a school in Duren, Westphalia, and, as well as maintaining the existing contacts in France and America, exchanged correspondence, albums and magazines with schools in Holland and New Zealand. At the same time, and emphasising that it was still essentially a country grammar school, Governors received in 1950 a letter from the local Agricultural Executive Committee "suggesting that (they) . . . be asked to consider fixing school holidays to fit in with agricultural needs and stating that for the potato harvest in this district the first or second week in October would be most suitable."

This was the great age of school societies – there were even concerns that there were too many and that they were competing for members and vacant evenings. Mr Newby's enthusiasm lay behind much of this but his health was giving increasing concern. In 1951 Mr. Evans, the Senior Master, retired. The County ruling was that henceforth in mixed schools the Senior Mistress ranked after the Headmaster. This was Miss Brown who, in the increasingly frequent absences of Mr Newby, thus became the first woman to be in charge. The mixed school was now thoroughly established and the patronising air which had characterised early attitudes had gone; indeed by 1950 there were 211 girls to 180 boys. At the same time Governors had concerns that, of an intake of 82 pupils, only 23 were from Ilkley and its immediate district, and that this figure had been falling for several years. As the County pointed out, this was not unduly alarming when the extent of the catchment area was considered, for "the area deemed to be served by the School includes the townships of Addingham, Denton, Middleton, Bolton Abbey, Ilkley, Burley-in-Wharfedale and Menston."

The 5th and 6th Form Christmas Dance in 1952. Mr Newby was able to attend in his wheelchair.

In 1951 Mr Bartle, known affectionately as 'Tubby', retired. He had enjoyed a long career at the School, having been appointed by Mr Frazer in 1918. He chose, as a leaving present, a bench vice, which gave rise to the following valediction in the Olicanian:

TUBBY'S TEMPTATION

After too many years of tedious virtue
Did it suddenly occur to you
That now, at last, it would be rather nice
To indulge in a little harmless vice?

In one of history's odd coincidences, the same issue of the magazine announced the appointment of Eric Whitaker who was to serve the School for exactly the same length of time, retiring as Senior Master and Head of Sixth Form in 1984. Thus in two abutting careers were written sixty-six years of history, from a boys' grammar school with boarders to a mixed comprehensive school.

The Queen's coronation in 1953 produced a flurry of celebrations. A Coronation Concert raised £25 for the King George VI Memorial Fund. Souvenir beakers (for the seniors) and mugs (for the juniors) were presented by the Chairman of the Urban District Council. The whole school walked down to the Grove Cinema to see the Coronation Newsreel and then enjoyed a

A presentation to Mr Evans (Senior Master) on his retirement in 1951. Miss Brown (Senior Mistress) is on the far left. Behind her is Head Boy D. Dickinson. On the right are Mr Newby and Head Girl Kathleen Bubb.

Mr Evans was appointed to the School in 1911 and was the only teacher to have a school society named after him - the R.W. Evans Chess Club.

A visit to the Festival of Britain in 1951.

picnic and dance. The most imaginative activity was the creation of the Coronation Cairn. Gordon McLachlan, another teacher who continued well into comprehensive days, prepared and carved a centre pole which was then ceremonially erected on the skyline of the Moor. A tin box was filled with "topical souvenirs" and buried by the pole. A party of sixth formers had prepared the foundations and the school then trekked up the hillside to make their contributions of stones. Thus was the Coronation Cairn created. There was another picnic on the slope behind White Wells and the afternoon continued with the singing of "appropriate songs." Unfortunately it rained and the programme was curtailed, thus preventing the cairn from reaching its intended height. This gave rise to the steely injunction: "All Olicanians, young and old, are asked to regard this Cairn as their collective responsibility and to make it a point of honour to contribute to it whenever they pass that way." Whether it continued to grow and how long it remained in place are not known.

Mr Newby was in poor health for many years and it is a tribute to his perseverance and his sense of duty that he was able to accomplish so much. Towards the end he was in hospital for long periods and was confined to a wheelchair in school. When he was unable to attend Governors' meetings, rather than simply deliver a

The Coronation Pole 1953. The pole is planted and the tin box is placed in the cairn.

written report, he chose to tape record his comments. He died on 19th September 1954. The concluding sentence of the tribute paid to him will serve as his epitaph: "He made it truly a school for boys *and* girls."

His successor was Felix Alan Walbank, Head of English at The City of Norwich School and an old boy of Bradford Grammar School. He was appointed in December 1954 and took up his post in May 1955. Almost immediately he and the Governors were plunged into protracted negotiations over playing fields. Provision had been inadequate ever since the advent of the mixed school in 1939 and by the early 1950s the cost of hiring additional facilities was over £100 a year. In 1950 the use was suggested of land bought before the war as a site for a Modern School but now

A School trip to Austria in 1953.

From the back row, left to right: Butler, Rita Shaw, Erica Dale, Jean King, V. Hartley, Tim Robinson, Lacy, Vivienne Pedley, Pat Jarman, Dale Hartley, Mr & Mrs Bilsby, Joy Bentley, J. Hinchcliffe, Jil Fountain, June Outhwaite, P. Bell, Miss Graves, Pat Hewitt, Turnbull, Mr & Mrs Nutter, Jen Leach, Ed Birrell, Preston, Teasdill.

Felix Alan Walbank, Headmaster from 1955 to 1965.

(unaccountably) not required for that purpose. The Governors declined "as it would mean the School having three separate playing fields all in a district surrounded by housing property and open to damage and vandalism such as the Governors are already experiencing in their present fields in the same vicinity." Then the Ilkley Agricultural Society suggested they might like to lease the land next to Ben Rhydding Hockey Club but that, for the moment, came to nothing. Finally the Governors wondered whether the County would be prepared to improve the land next to the school site, the additional five acres purchased in 1925 for a girls' grammar school, which continued unused. In particular they wanted an architect "to submit a scheme for the levelling of that field to make one pitch at the bottom and tennis courts at the top end." The tennis courts were, of course, eventually provided.

The possibility of long-term improvement came with the acquisition by the Urban District Council of fifteen acres of land at Wheatley Holme, next to the Ben Rhydding Sports Club. The idea was that the Grammar School would sell its two playing fields in Valley Drive for building land. In return the Council would replace them by leasing the land at Wheatley Holme. This would entail a slightly longer journey for Games lessons (there were even mutterings that it would make every match seem like an 'away' game) but the overall area was larger and it would ensure adequate provision for both girls' and boys' teams. The Governors favoured the idea but there were problems. First the Education Committee wanted "to consider the views of all educational bodies in Ilkley to ascertain the full details of requirements for land in Ilkley for future educational developments." Then the Ministry of Education weighed into the debate by stating the fifteen acres were unnecessary and that it considered nine to ten acres sufficient for the School's needs. It was therefore suggested that Wheatley Holme might be shared with the new Secondary School, but the Grammar School Governors were having none of that. Then there was the question of a pavilion. It was the Local Authority's responsibility to provide one but the Governors wanted something better than the standard model. Providence intervened when the wall dividing the school site from the additional five acres was pronounced unsafe. Rather than pay £300 to mend it, the Governors took the pragmatic decision to knock it down and store the stones for a new pavilion. From this time the five acres, which had previously been reserved for

The Board of Governors 1953 - 54.

1953-54
ILKLEY GRAMMAR SCHOOL

Recognised by the Board of Education
as a Secondary School   No. 8:72

BOARD OF GOVERNORS under Scheme of 24th June, 1909

Chairman - - Councillor G. W. Clough

Co-optative Governors	First Appointment	Present Appointment terminates
P. Dalton	1939	
C. Thompson	1950	April, 1957
Mrs. A. L. Davidson, M.A.	1941	
R. S. Dower, M.A.	1921	
Dr. Dorothy Farrar, B.A.	1946	Feb., 1956

Representative Governors appointed by—
West Riding County Council

J. H. Armistead, M.A., C.Ald.	1925	
H. Eagle	1937	July, 1955
S. Ryder Runton	1951	
Mrs. J. S. Thorp	1947	

Ilkley Urban District Council

Mrs. D. I. Wray	1951	
G. W. Clough	1945	March, 1954
W. Hill	1951	
Mrs. F. Hampshire	1942	
Mrs. H. Hawkins	1949	
J. Hardy	1949	March, 1955
J. H. Bowes	1952	

Wharfedale Rural District Council

J. W. Layfield	1952	March, 1955

Leeds University

Prof. J LePatourel, M.A ,D.Phil.	1952	Nov., 1953

Headmaster—J. S. Newby, M.A.   Tel. 65

Treasurer—H. Craven, Barclays Bank, Ltd.

Clerk to the Governors—C. Anderson, A.C.C.S.
Divisional Education Officer
Otley. Tel Otley 2621

grazing, had even been ploughed up during the war and had consequently remained out-of-bounds, began to be used for games and practices. What is left of the wall still stands at the top of the school site near the 'Exit' gate on Cowpasture Road.

It took a number of years for the matter to be resolved. The Grammar School decided it could just about manage with a ten acre field, though it would mean abandoning plans for four hard tennis courts. However it maintained that the ten acres should be for its exclusive use, leaving the remainder of the land for the Authority to lease to the Secondary School, though in practice there was some sharing. The proceeds of the sale of the old fields were to be put towards the cost of a custom-built pavilion. The initial estimate of £10,000 was, as ever, inadequate, and at a final cost of £12,000 (minus £350 for the wall stones) the Governors got pretty much the pavilion they wanted. There was a sense of nostalgia when the last Sports Day was held at the old field in May 1962. When it had been acquired in 1904 it had been in open country; now it was a green oasis in a residential area. Soon it was to accommodate the grey monolith of the International Wool Secretariat. The final act saw the old pavilion, Mr Atkinson's pride and joy, demolished in 1964.

The front of the School in the 1950s.

By 1955 there were 182 boys and 254 girls, and pupils were travelling from as far afield as Guiseley and Horsforth. The Chief Education Officer for the West Riding was the legendary Sir Alec Clegg and across the area there was a sense of optimism and enlightenment. The Grammar School was, of course, selective, only those passing the 11-plus exam being qualified to attend. Thus it was assured of a constant supply of able pupils and there was a real sense of continuity and certainty about its work. The Olicanian, as ever, gives a window onto this world. The house system continued, societies proliferated, detailed results of the many teams were faithfully chronicled, the 'Valete' section gave a potted history of each leaver, there was the usual mix of articles and reports and the Old Olicanians' supplement recorded news and events such as the Annual Dinner and the Christmas Dance. For several years the School provided child singers for Covent Garden Opera Company productions in Leeds. There were dances and debates, foreign visits and field courses and even (a sign of the times) a Balloon Debate featuring Brigitte Bardot and Elvis Presley. The Coutances Exchange blossomed. In 1956 M. Lechaptois distributed the annual awards on a glorious July day on the front lawn. He revelled in his status as an honorary Englishman:

> On certain occasions, in Coutances, some of you scholars saw me wearing the school tie and you thought I was entitled to do so. Indeed I joined the Grammar School ten years ago when, co-operating with Mr Swallow, I started the Ilkley – Coutances visits.

He cautioned against national stereotypes by mocking them:

> When abroad people say, "Ça, c'est bien anglais!" they usually mean it's tweedy, dowdy, loose-limbed, clean-cut, lantern-jawed, long-toothed, fair, somewhat arrogant, supercilious, athletic, squeamish, easily shocked, unimaginative, devoid of any taste in art, food or wines, ever clamouring for tea, toast or baths . . . Some English believe the average Frenchman fears fresh air in the house almost as much as water on his body. They say that the few bathrooms one may happen to find are seldom connected to any water supply. It is well-known that the French feed exclusively on snails and frogs. Their cooking is so devilishly sophisticated that they will turn these loathsome reptiles into excellent steaks, cutlets and chops. The only thing they do not attempt to disguise is garlic.

At the same time there were concerns. In 1958 the Scout Troop, founded in the 1920s and re-constituted in 1947 by Norman Salmon, ceased because nobody could be found to help to run it. The Old Olicanians too were beginning to feel changed times; only a fraction of those eligible were joining and there were serious doubts about whether events like the Christmas Dance could continue. Even the magazine was having trouble drumming up contributions. In other parts of the country the first comprehensive schools were being established. In truth, the world was changing though it may not have seemed so at the time. Other links with the past were severed. In 1954 Mr Bartle died. In 1960 the School was shocked by the death of Mr Swallow. There was a tragic event in 1959 when the Head Boy, David Priestman, was killed by a rock fall in an underground passage at Dow Cave near Kettlewell.

On 6th December 1960 the new Ilkley Secondary School on Valley Drive was occupied for the first time. It was a purpose-built school designed to replace the hotch-potch of buildings pressed into service in recent years, though the accommodation in the old building on Bolling Road continued to be needed. The new school was formally opened by The Countess of Scarborough on 11th December 1961. Mr Brabban remained as Head until 1968 when he was succeeded by Mr E.R. Schirn, who remained as Head until April 1970. Mary Weatherall was then in charge until July 1970, before moving, with a number of other staff, to the comprehensive Grammar School. In its short history the Valley Drive building was linked to the Grammar School in a variety of ways. For ten years the two schools provided secondary education in the area. When comprehensive education was introduced in 1970, they amalgamated on the Cowpasture Road site, with the Secondary School becoming Ilkley Middle School. When the two-tier system returned in 2000, it was, for three years, the Grammar School's 11-13 Lower School, before being demolished in 2003.

Change was in the air on another front. The inadequacies of the Grammar School building had long been recognised. Apart from the swimming pool, there had been only a few piecemeal additions since Mr Swann's extensions of 1898 – a dining hut, a Domestic Science unit, two external classrooms, an improved library and

The School Hall in the 1950s. By this time the old 'Big School' of 1893 had become inadequate and it was replaced in 1964. The overcrowding is evident.

some girls' cloakrooms. The accommodation was simply not up to the demands of the brave new world of the 1960s. The Hall was still the old 'Big School' of 1893. There was a shortage of properly equipped science labs. Dining arrangements were primitive. The gym was small and old-fashioned, with the most basic changing facilities. The staffroom was barely adequate.

The early omens were not good. In January 1957 sketch plans of suggested alterations and extensions submitted to the County Authority were airily dismissed:

> The Assistant Education Officer has seen the Headmaster, and he has given him to understand that a major project such as this stands next to no chance of getting into a building programme, both from the point of view of our own priorities and the Ministry of Education restrictions.

The Authority, while appreciating the need for extra accommodation, wanted to provide only 'West Riding' rooms, a euphemism for more huts. But the Governors stood firm, and by 1959, after two years of painstaking negotiation, they had what they wanted. Mr Walbank was able to announce at the Speech Day in November 1960:

In this coming year I hope and expect we may see the beginning of the School's development to its full establishment size. A building plan has been approved and a sum of money, something over £100,000, has been earmarked. Of what will the development consist? First of all there is to be a new Assembly Hall large enough to take the whole school. Alongside it there will be a new large Gymnasium with proper changing accommodation and showers. A School Kitchen will make it possible to cook and supply midday meals on the spot with proper seating for it in the hall. These buildings will be linked to our present one by an entrance lobby at the end of our present Assembly Hall. For special teaching rooms we expect a new full-sized Biology Laboratory, a new Woodwork Shop and by

Mr Walbank and Staff in 1957.

Back row l to r: Mr Bracken, Mr Nutter, Mr Stafford, Mr Cresswell, Mr Pollard, Mr McMachlen, Mr Birch,
Middle Row l to r: Mr Hawkesworth, Mr Bilsby, Miss Wilde, Miss Edwards, Miss Heap (Secretary), Miss Pfeffer (American exchange teacher for Miss Croft), Mr Ward, Mr Whitaker.
Front Row l to r: Miss Bridgens, Mrs Walker, Miss Graham, Mr Walbank, Mr Swallow, Mr Walker Mr Salmon. (Absent: Miss Jackson and Mr Harrison).

A school uniform advert from 1951.

conversion of sub-standard classrooms and other spaces, a proper Music Room and an enlarged Art Room. All this will mean that the existing boys' playground will become an enclosed courtyard, and so what were originally cloisters but have since been made into the woodwork room, will revert again to cloisters as in 1893.

There was to be new accommodation for medical inspections, for sixth form study groups, for the staff, for the secretary – and even for the Headmaster, who concluded that "Ilkley Grammar School will in this fourth century of its existence become four square in plan and fully equipped by modern standards." The cost was

£145,000, including £18,000 for furniture and equipment.

In July 1961 the hard work began. There were massive extensions on the east side and the Caretaker's house was suddenly perched on a precipice. Lessons were accompanied by the din of pile-drivers securing the supports for the new hall. When the first set of pillars were found to have been wrongly aligned they had to be destroyed and replaced. Norman Salmon remembered 1962:

> We sought shelter in room after room, and struggled hard and successfully to work. No gym, no swimming bath. Oil heaters, classes in the ATC hut, form prayers, no school assembly, the daily room change programme. Mud – the Domestic Science room and the Dining Hut reached through trenches, past bulldozers, cement-mixers and tar boilers. And always - somewhere - noise.

Joyce McBurney was appointed School Secretary in 1962, a post she filled for twenty-five years before becoming Clerk to the Governors. She remembered her first summer:

> In the summer of 1962 work began in earnest. I think if I had known the chaos that was to ensue during my first summer holidays (I worked all year round, not term-time only) I might not have accepted the job quite so rapturously. The entrance hall was being altered so I had to climb over piles of rubble each morning to reach my office. The dust and noise were unbelievable. One morning I arrived to find a mini-bulldozer in the hall. Enough was enough! The weather was glorious so I asked the caretaker to move my desk and chair to the front lawn and I worked there. One day I was busily typing class lists under the shade of a walnut tree when the Divisional Education Officer arrived. With a grin he observed that I should be paying the LEA for the privilege of working in such surroundings.

The Olicanian tried to be philosophical:

> During the past twelve months, new shapes have been growing up around us and the old outline of the school is changing. The birth pangs of this newness we all know – need we recall the mud, the persistent drone of machinery, the mud, the clanging, banging and yelling, the mud. . . and the dust. Perhaps we have learned a little of patience and fortitude through this experience.

Exams had to be taken in the ballroom of the Stoney Lea Hotel. A lorry packed with bricks stuck in the mud for several days to the delight of small boys. "Why not burn it instead of burying it, mate?" suggested a visiting fire-officer. The start of the Autumn Term had to be delayed. The foundations became flooded and days and nights were punctuated by the throb of the pumps. The gym's new roof covering blew off one night, depositing itself in nearby gardens. Yet in spite of everything the work was duly completed. There were generous donations. Percy Dalton (Mr Atkinson's one hundredth pupil) gave the organ, a two-manual Compton which had begun life in the chapel at Rudding Park and on which Arthur Pickett gave a recital on the afternoon of the opening. Cedric Thompson provided the lectern and Mrs A.L. Davidson, a former governor, a grand piano. Seating for spectators at the swimming pool was given by the Parents' Association. On 7th March 1964 the extensions were formally opened by the Princess Royal.

There were other changes. For some time the Old Olicanians had been ailing. The Association, so vibrant for so many years, was withering through lack of support. For some, according to an editorial of 1964, the reason was clear:

The Princess Royal, accompanied by County Alderman W. Hyman, opens the building extensions on 7th March 1964.

We almost hesitate to mention that there still exists among diehards the feeling that the Association should never have attempted to cope with both Old Boys and Old Girls and would have a much better opportunity of succeeding as two separate Associations.

In a letter dramatically headed "Euthanasia or Plastic Surgery?" the situation was laid bare:

The AGM on 19th March 1964 instructed the Committee to ask every member whether the Association should die mercifully, or whether enough support will be forthcoming to revitalise it. We are in the process of throwing in the towel and calling off the losing battle. It would be a pity to see it die after so many years, but even the most enthusiastic get discouraged when their efforts bear no fruit.

Mr Walbank and Staff - 1964.

The rallying cry had little effect. At an Extraordinary General Meeting on 18th March 1965 the Association was suspended with a caretaker committee and, in effect, ceased to exist.

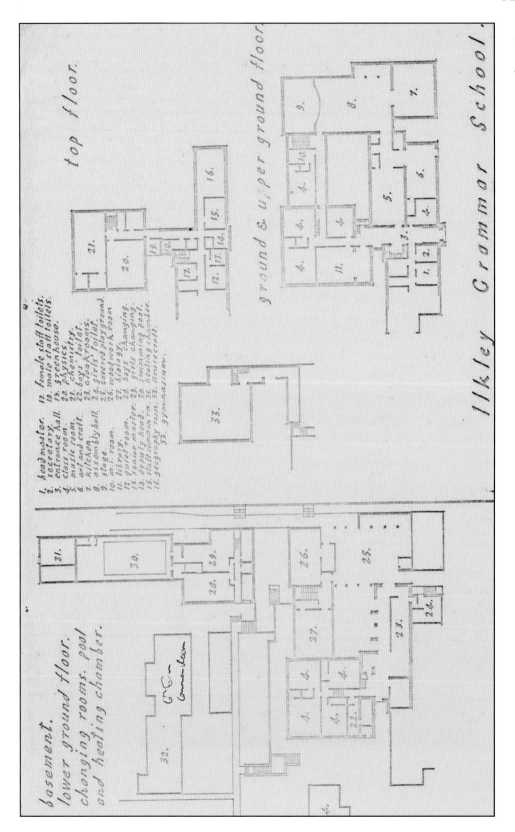

*A plan of the
building
following the
1964
extensions.*

Ilkley Grammar School.

ground & upper ground floor.

top floor.

1. headmaster.
2. secretary.
3. entrance hall.
4. class room.
5. music room.
6. art and craft.
7. kitchen.
8. assembly hall.
9. stage.
10. mit room.
11. library.
12. junior room.
13. senior master.
14. deputy head.
15. staff common rm.
16. geography room.
17. female staff toilets.
18. male staff toilets.
19. greenhouse.
20. physics.
21. chemistry.
22. boys toilet.
23. cloakrooms.
24. girls toilet.
25. covered playground.
26. woodwork room.
27. biology.
28. boys changing.
29. girls changing.
30. swimming pool.
31. heating chamber.
32. handicraft.
33. gymnasium.

basement.
lower ground floor.
changing rooms. pool
and heating chamber.

In August 1965 Mr Walbank resigned and, until a successor could be appointed, Norman Salmon became Acting Head. When, the following year, Mr J.H. Douglas took up the post, Mr Salmon drew an elegant historical parallel by saying that the School "had had enough of the Commonwealth and were looking forward to the Restoration." In fact it was a brief interlude for in 1967 Mr Douglas returned to Cumberland for family reasons. He was succeeded in 1968 by Richard Hughes, Head of History at Ifield Comprehensive School, West Sussex, the last incumbent to occupy the Headmaster's house, and that for only a year. Thus, as Tony Barringer points out, the School, which had had only five Heads since 1893 now had three in the space of three years. One of Mr Walbank's last appointments was Miss Pearson who was to be the Deputy Head for the next nineteen years. As ever, links with the past were severed. In 1965 Mr Evans died. He had been Senior Mathematics Master from 1911 to 1951, spending all but three of his teaching years at Ilkley. The tribute to him in the Olicanian, while specific to "Chuff" Evans, can also be said to stand for a generation of teachers:

> It is always difficult to know just how a man can become legendary in his own time, but this "Chuff" Evans certainly did. He was respected as a fine teacher, even by mathematical imbeciles, and, despite his stern, somewhat remote manner, was always thought of with affection.

The Upper Sixth in 1966. In the front row are Miss Pearson (Senior Mistress), Mr Douglas (Headmaster) and Mr Salmon (Senior Master).

Perhaps it was that he represented the epitome of the old guard of schoolmasters, with his stoop, tattered, chalky gown and predatory appearance. His idiosyncrasies, especially the deliberate mistakes, were always appreciated with relish.

The world was changing and, though it may not have realised it, the Grammar School was living through its last selective years. Some of the recollections of the fifties and sixties seem like echoes from a distant past: the ritual toasts of the Swann Boys, the Atkinson Boys and the Frazer Boys at the Old Olicanians' dinners; the strict rules regarding the wearing by girls of berets; the singing of the School Song at Speech Day; the whole school walking to the local church for the Carol Service; the shredding and even burning of the striped blazers as boys moved into the fourth year; the very real inter-house rivalry. Now new forces were at work which would re-shape very rapidly the educational landscape of the country. Not for the first time the School would need to adapt to changing times.

Comprehensive or Apprehensive?

Comprehensive schools were not a new idea in the 1960s. They had been proposed in the 1944 Education Act and had been introduced in parts of London and Wales during the 1950s. They were given fresh impetus by the election of a Labour government in 1964 and by widespread dissatisfaction with the operation of the 11-plus examination. It was argued that it was quite wrong to make decisions at eleven about which type of school a child should attend. Mistakes were made which could not be rectified, the process was socially divisive and there were concerns about the effectiveness of some of the secondary modern schools. The Government declared its objective to end selection in a motion passed in January 1965, noting with approval "the efforts of local authorities to reorganise secondary education on comprehensive lines, which will preserve all that is valuable in grammar school education for those children who now receive it and make it available to more children. The Government recognises that the method and timing of such organisation should vary to meet local needs and believes that the time is now ripe for a declaration of national policy." The Department of Education and Science was then instructed to prepare schemes for the national reorganisation of secondary education. This resulted in Circular 10/65 which provided guidance on the methods by which comprehensive education could be achieved. Six possible schemes were suggested, though in practice three were most common: the orthodox 11-18 school, a system of middle and upper schools, and 11-16 schools feeding into a sixth form college. This, then, was very much a centrally-driven process and it was a very rapid development. In 1968 approximately 20 per cent of secondary schools were comprehensive. By 1975 the changes had been almost fully implemented.

The new Headmaster, Mr Hughes, was under no doubt that he was "appointed to tackle reorganisation." This meant nothing less than the amalgamation of the Grammar School and the

Richard (Dick) Hughes, Headmaster from 1968 to 1979.

Secondary School. However, instead of taking pupils at 11, the new school was to sit atop a three-tier pyramid of First, Middle and Upper and hence would not take them until they were 13 and entering the Third Year. There was also the inevitable building work. This time there was greater urgency, for the new school, still to be called Ilkley Grammar, was to open in 1971. Hence, barely five years after one difficult building programme, another, potentially more complex, was set to begin. Mr Hughes recognised the problem at once: "Having just survived all that (the new Hall etc.) it was hard that they were being pitchforked so soon into a second upheaval potentially much more disruptive and disturbing than the first."

Initially things went well, so well that the completion date was brought forward to 1970. "It was a common wisecrack of the time," said Mr Hughes, "that schools were either comprehensive or apprehensive and this shortening of the period of apprehension seemed a good idea." Then the problems began. There were the inevitable, endless discussions with architects and resulting modifications to the original plan. The siting of the Sports Hall turned out to be contentious, for it blocked the view of the Moor from the Coronation Hospital. Then the builders went bankrupt. It soon became clear that there was no chance of the buildings being ready for September 1970 but by now it was too late to revert to the original date. The anxiety and uncertainty were voiced in the Olicanian:

> The last term of Ilkley Grammar School as we have known it is nearing its close. As many of us look back, staff and pupils alike, we cannot but feel a little sadness, but at the same time a sense of pride that we have been privileged to share in the life of such a fine school. We have great hopes and expectations, however. Preparations for the new School have involved a great expenditure of time, thought and energy. There have been snags. Work on the new buildings was halted several weeks ago and has only just recommenced. The opening of the new facilities may be delayed, and the life of the School in the meantime may not be easy; but we are sure that in due course the new School will show that all the efforts that went into its making were thoroughly worthwhile.

The only solution was to find additional short-term accommodation; the nearest available was at Bolling Road and so, for two terms, the School became split-site. There was anxiety on this count as well:

Looking ahead to September, most of the School feel rather apprehensive, particularly next year's second and third formers who will be going to the Bolling Road School for at least the early part of the school year. Once the new term starts we are sure this feeling will quickly disappear, and that everyone will respond vigorously to the challenges and opportunities which the new School offers.

I LEFT AT THIS POINT !

The staff weren't too enamoured of it either. Arthur Palmer christened it "Bollers" and "Bollers" it remained. Jean and Andrew Lambert recalled, "A hard core of young and supposedly resilient staff was based there, with a few more experienced teachers to stabilise us." They went on to recall life at "Bollers":

The staffroom was like a Victorian third-class railway compartment. Long and thin, it had two rows of chairs facing each other down the sides. Every morning the Head, Mr Hughes, would phone with details of the daily staff meeting in an effort to keep us in touch with what was going on at the main site. We all tried to be as far away from the phone as possible to avoid having to answer it. The details were relayed to the rest of the staff who sat facing each other, grinning facetiously at the poor soul who had picked up the phone.

Mr. Hughes reported to Governors, "Being straddled between this and the Bolling Road site is a nuisance. The children move only after assembly and during break and the dinner hour but the weather seems to keep its sharpest showers for the hour when we have most in transit and some children are remarkably loath to bring proper protective clothing."

The building work was considerable and not everything went to plan. Still in a skeletal stage, the framework was buckled by heavy winds and had to be corrected and strengthened before work could continue. In effect a four-storey extension was being fitted to the 1964 rooms, marching in a northerly direction down the hill towards Springs Lane. The top floor housed an extension to the library, the new staffroom and two smaller rooms, the second floor a suite of laboratories, the first floor had rooms for Art, Home Economics, Needlework and Pottery, while the ground floor had a second hall which doubled as a dining room, plus a kitchen and several classrooms. There was a smaller two-floor extension to the west containing several offices and two classrooms. The original plan to build a Creative Arts block at the top of the site near Cowpasture Road had to be shelved because of expense and instead a more modest single storey open-plan suite of four rooms for Woodwork, Metalwork, Design and Art was built just below the new extension two years later. The bulk of the work was completed by Easter 1971, when the two-term sojourn at "Bollers" came to an end. The Grammar School was once more reunited on one site, this time as a 13-18 Upper School and the new buildings were officially opened by Sir Alec Clegg. The whole process had been a difficult one for the staff, for not only had they to cope with the building work and the split site, but the new school felt a curious animal, with two years simply lopped off. It was hard for those who particularly enjoyed teaching the younger pupils and there had to be flexibility to cater for individual preferences. Elsewhere there were similar adjustments to be made. The primary schools had, in changing to first schools, lost their two oldest year groups.

In the new arrangement there were to be six first schools. The Addingham school replaced the old 'High' School built on Chapel Street in 1874. It opened in 1967, was extended in 1975 and eventually demolished in 2001, following the latest schools' reorganisation. In Ilkley there were three first schools, All Saints, housed in what had been the old National School of 1872, Bolling Road, which had opened in 1909 as an elementary school for Ben Rhydding and seen life in a variety of subsequent guises, and

The back of the building prior to the 1970 extensions.

Ashlands, which had opened as an infants' school in 1953. There were two first schools in Burley. Burley C of E, on Aireville Terrace, had opened as an elementary school in 1898 and had become an infant and junior school in 1950. At the time of the 1970 reorganisation the Head was Frank Newbould, an Old Olicanian and a Grammar School governor. Burley and Woodhead School had the longest history of all, having opened in 1832. However, by the 1970s, the building was no longer large enough and a replacement was opened in 1976 next to the newly-built Sandholme estate. The old building still remains at the top of Moor Lane. The 9-13 Middle Schools were an entirely new concept. At first there were two of them, in Ilkley (where the Secondary School buildings were taken over) and in Burley, whose children were taught first in Ilkley and then in a variety of accommodation around the village until the new school on Langford Lane was completed in 1973. In 1979 a third middle school opened, in Addingham, which also drew pupils from the west of Ilkley.

There were other changes as the new Grammar School moved into the 1970s. The green blazers, replaced by what were felt to be more modern-looking and less expensive sweaters, became the subject of great nostalgia. The house system assumed its final (and brief) form with the introduction of Heber, Middleton, Rombald and Wheatley. The Olicanian was published for the last time in 1971. First produced in 1900, it had, perhaps, run its course and, like some other aspects of school life, was felt to belong to a past generation. Certainly the paucity of material written for it was a constant theme of editorials in later years. It had remained a faithful chronicle for almost three quarters of a century and was not effectively replaced until the advent of the Newsletter twenty years later. Its last Editorial summed up the transition:

> Our first year as a Comprehensive School has not been an easy one. Any period of transition presents problems, and we have certainly had our share. The new buildings not being ready, innumerable difficulties were caused by the School's having to be divided between Bolling Road and Cowpasture Road. From September to April, second- and third-formers and staff alike were to be seen hurrying along Bolling Road, trying to keep up with their timetables. This often proved impossible; teachers had to leave lessons early or arrive late at the next one. The winter weather did not help matters, and pupils often reached the School cold, wet, and bedraggled-looking. Now, however, we are all together and beginning at last to feel a real entity.

The difficulties facing the new school were considerable. The union between grammar and secondary had been forced rather than sought. It retained the 'Grammar School' name, as, curiously, did a number of comprehensives in the area. There were those who felt that was wrong, either because the name was too strongly associated with selection and was in any case an inaccurate title or because there remained a strong sense of loyalty to the memory of the old school and it was felt a new one should have a new name. On the other hand there was a sense of familiarity and pride in "the Grammar School" and so "the Grammar School" it remained. For the staff there were the challenges of teaching pupils who spanned a much broader range than they were used to or, in some cases, were even trained to teach. Those least affected, in a way, were the pupils who were, after all, simply rubbing shoulders with those they had been with since the age of five. But the School, shorn of its first two years, had a different 'feel'. There were those on the staff who preferred the more mature ethos, the absence of the shrill voices of the young; but there were those who felt it to be in some way incomplete without them. It certainly shifted the balance of teaching as, suddenly, a greater proportion of pupils were being prepared for external examinations.

For all the new comprehensives at this time there was a balance to be struck between maintaining continuity and starting afresh. The watchword was "the best of the old and the best of the new" but this was a difficult balance to achieve. The maintenance of the house system, for instance, could be seen as a continuation of good practice or anachronistic. To retain the old uniform could be seen as an unwillingness to adapt; to change it (especially from a blazer to a sweater) might seem like lowering standards. There were many such issues, as individual schools sought to carve out a new and appropriate identity for themselves. And of course, always, in the background there were the alternatives. Just up the road at Skipton there was still selective education. In Leeds and Bradford there were grammar schools which stood outside the state system and had been unaffected by the recent changes. It wasn't easy for parents to make informed choices. Examination results were not published in any kind of standard form and there were no regular inspection reports.

Nevertheless, in such challenging circumstances the new Grammar School made its way. The curriculum was broadened to include practical subjects such as Horticulture and Vehicle Maintenance. Integrated Studies students attended link courses at local colleges. Plays, 'Camelot', 'Oh, What a Lovely War' and others, usually produced by David Wildman, became a regular attraction. One of the immediate benefits of the larger school was the growth of the School Orchestra. There were carol services at the Parish Church and concerts each April. There was now a Creative Studies Department led by Ivan Minto who recalls:

> The major events were the Creative Studies Evenings, when entertainment was provided by the Music Department in the Sports Hall, there were exhibitions and demonstrations in the Needlework, Art and Craft areas, there was quality dining in the Library and, to finish, Drama in the Hall.

Games teams flourished, with the appointment of keen young staff and augmented by the larger pool of players. The Sixth Form, with Eric Whitaker as Head, continued to grow and moved into its new Centre, having had to put up for some time with Ilkley Youth Club for its 'lunchtime relaxation'. A Youth Tutor was appointed to liaise between the School and other organisations. Two successful EYE Days (Explore Your Environment) were organised, which involved everyone doing a walk or run of appropriate length for charity. The Summer Programme (a three-day activities programme in July, abbreviated ingloriously to SUMP) was introduced and included such exotic pursuits as rail-roving, bottle digging and bee-keeping (the latter in Mr. Hughes' garden). The School raised the money for two Land Rovers which three staff drove to Africa. Of course there were familiar activities. The Coutances exchange continued unabated; it reached its 30th anniversary in 1977, having been elevated in 1969 into a formal twinning between the towns. The Old Olicanians may have ceased but a tradition of informal reunions was begun in 1971 when a group of girls who had left ten years earlier met for dinner at the Craiglands. The Parents' Association, which had been wound up in 1969, was re-formed for the new upper school and was soon in business raising money and arranging tours of the new building. There was a staff cricket team which was still going strong twenty five years later. There were even attempts to re-establish a magazine. One simply called "I" ran to four editions, styling itself "An anthology of creative and critical work and comments on school life by the pupils and staff." One edition included a debate about the merits of comprehensive education, and another about whether or not exam results should be published (the School had always resisted pressure to do so).

Those who hoped the building work had been completed were to be disappointed for in 1972 the leaving age was raised from 15 to 16. This required additional accommodation, so five more rooms were created, four in one block and the fifth the curious octagonal room which became known affectionately as 'The Thre'penny Bit'. But these were relatively minor works compared to what had gone before and the school site had now assumed the layout which was to serve it for almost thirty years.

A further change came on 1ˢᵗ April 1974 with the reorganisation of local government. The West Riding, especially under the leadership of Sir Alec Clegg, was regarded with a degree of affection rarely accorded to education authorities. Sir Alec had been a teacher, he had written books about teaching and he knew how schools worked. Now the West Riding was to disappear and the towns along the Wharfe valley were swallowed up by the new enlarged urban authorities. Otley became part of Leeds; Ilkley, perhaps surprisingly, was included in Bradford. It wasn't an easy transfer for the School, steeped as it was in West Riding tradition. It had to find a role for itself in a new local authority in which it was far from being a typical school.

Beneath all this, there were uneasy rumblings on the national scene. As early as 1971 there was the start of a backlash against comprehensive schools. Two academics, Brian Cox and A.E. Dyson published the 'Black Papers' in which they criticised standards and behaviour in the new schools. 'Child-centred education', one of the mantras of the sixties, was beginning to come under fire. Then the papers were full of horror stories from William Tyndale School in Islington, where the head ran the school as a co-operative and told a governor he "didn't give a damn about parents." As the evangelical zeal for comprehensives began to run out of steam, questions were increasingly asked about whether there was any coherence in what they were trying to achieve. Shortly after becoming Prime Minister in 1976, James Callaghan seized the moment. His speech at Ruskin College, Oxford was a seminal point in English education. Up to then it had been axiomatic that the government did not interfere in state education. It might adjust the structure from time to time but what went on in the classroom was left to the schools. All that changed in 1976. There were no immediate practical effects but the climate of discussion was never the same again. What he said, were it repeated today, would seem unexceptional. Then it was revolutionary. There were, he said, complaints from parents and employers about the level of educational attainment of a significant number of school leavers. There were concerns about "the new informal methods of teaching." It was no good, he said, producing socially well-adjusted young people who didn't have the necessary skills. He listed areas where he wanted further discussion. There was "a strong case for the so-called core curriculum of basic knowledge" and the "proper way of monitoring the use of resources in order to maintain a proper national standard of performance." He wanted to look afresh at the examination system, at provision for the less academic and at the relationship between industry and education.

Schools, not unnaturally, saw it as a threat. The Guardian predicted, "Shudders will be seismically recorded in many teachers' common rooms today." Terry Casey, General Secretary of the National Association of Schoolmasters, bristled, "We would resist any attempt to turn teachers into educational navvies." Many teachers felt their professionalism was being questioned. Critics said teachers were being over-protective of the 'secret garden' of the curriculum. Throughout the late 1970s and into the 1980s battle lines were being drawn.

Ilkley Grammar School was going through more change. In 1979 Mr Hughes took up a post as a School Inspector in Derbyshire and Peter Wood, Deputy Head of Heaton School, Newcastle was appointed as Head. By now the School was an established comprehensive and the three-tier system, which had seemed so alien ten years earlier, was seen to bring a number of benefits. Because of its relative geographical isolation at the extremity of Bradford LEA, the Ilkley Pyramid was virtually self-contained, which meant there could be a high degree of liaison and hence continuity in what was taught. The schools knew each other well and parents had confidence in them. Each of the three communities had its own middle school and so children up to the age of 13 could be educated locally. The only exception was that a number from the west of Ilkley attended Addingham since there were never enough from the village to fill the school. Menston was a semi-detached member of the Pyramid; its children were still taught as infants and juniors and most continued to transfer at 11 into the Leeds secondary system, much to Bradford's disappointment. The three-tier Pyramid lasted for thirty years. Its popularity and success can be judged from the outcry which greeted eventual proposals that it should be replaced.

Technology was starting to make some jobs easier as, during the late 1970s, computers began to appear. The first machines at Ilkley, the PET Commodores, were large and heavy with a very small screen. Their range of tasks was limited although one, doing nothing more than ringing the bells at Parents' Evenings, almost made it to the 21st Century. By 1982 the School had its first computer room, equipped with the help of the Parents' Association. On the other hand, reprographic equipment had changed little in thirty years. Though the offset litho was developing in speed and reliability, the staple machine was still the Banda, with its messy blue ink and jamming drum. Word processors were not yet in common use and typewriters and carbon paper were still regularly employed for the production of copies. But progress was rapid and by 1984 there were not only word processors but improved printers, which revolutionised the

ILKLEY PYRAMID OF SCHOOLS

**ILKLEY
GRAMMAR SCHOOL**
Headteacher:
Mr P. N. Wood
Tel: 01943 608424

**ADDINGHAM
MIDDLE SCHOOL**
Headteacher:
Mr B. C. Hall
Tel: 01943 830944

**ILKLEY
MIDDLE SCHOOL**
Headteacher:
Mr G. D. Tee
Tel: 01943 608765

**BURLEY
MIDDLE SCHOOL**
Headteacher:
Mrs J. H. Rowe
Tel: 01943 862642

**BOLLING ROAD
FIRST SCHOOL**
Headteacher:
Mrs L. Davies
Tel: 01943 607648

**BURLEY & WOODHEAD
C.E. FIRST SCHOOL**
Headteacher:
Mrs S. H. Adsett
Tel: 01943 862739

**BURLEY
C.E. FIRST SCHOOL**
Headteacher:
Mr G. J. Edwards
Tel: 01943 863242

**ADDINGHAM
FIRST SCHOOL**
Headteacher:
Mrs J. E. Jones
Tel: 01943 830298

**ALL SAINTS
FIRST SCHOOL**
Headteacher:
Mr M. A. Carey
Tel: 01943 607852

**ASHLANDS
FIRST SCHOOL**
Headteacher:
Mrs G. Lofthouse
Tel: 01943 609050

THE PEAK OF
EDUCATIONAL OPPORTUNITY

In the 1980s and 1990s the Ilkley Pyramid of Schools advertised the linked provision it was able to make.

production of quality teaching materials and saved a lot of time. In 1981 the School Bank, organised with the Midland Bank, made its first appearance, staffed by sixth form students on the Business course. A Bradford report showed the School had one of the best Work Experience schemes in the District. Records of Achievement, designed to reflect more than just academic attainment, began to be developed. In 1986 changes were made to the school day, resulting in the earlier start and finish and shorter lunchtime which still operate.

The School Bank opens for custom in 1981.

These were not the only developments and, with the benefit of hindsight, it is possible to see the first glimmerings of what were to become major issues. As early as 1980, there were calls for Bradford to reorganise, this time at 16-plus. There were concerns over low participation rates and the limited range of courses in some schools. Although nothing came of it, and in any case Ilkley would probably have been immune, there was another motive: the need to save money. By 1981 Bradford Council was preparing a list of financial options for the coming year. They included cuts of 10% in capitation (the money allowed for books, stationery and equipment) and a reduction of 36 teaching posts. Throughout the

Authority, and not for the last time, pupil-teacher ratios worsened. At the same time a generous – and initially expensive – premature retirement scheme for teachers began to operate, and the Council was forced to give assurances that there would be no redundancies. It was the first spasm of the financial malaise which was to beset the Authority and its schools for the next twenty years. There were signs of other changes. For the first time a staff 'observer' was allowed into governors' meetings, exam results began to be collated by the Local Authority and published in a more consistent way and, more ominously, there was growing discontent among teachers that additional work and responsibilities were not being reflected in their salary structure.

The national debate Mr. Callaghan had wanted certainly took off; indeed it became known as 'The Great Debate'. At the same time schools were sucked into the prevailing national pessimism. The 'Winter of Discontent' in 1978-79 brought the Labour government down and swept Margaret Thatcher to power in May 1979. Immediately there was a much sharper policy towards trade unions and it was not long before schools began to feel the effects. In March 1982 one of the national teaching unions took 'industrial action' over a salary claim. This involved a withdrawal from voluntary activities and the closure of the School at lunchtime and, while it lasted only three weeks, it was the precursor to a much longer period of disruption. The major national confrontation was the miners' strike in 1984, during which coal stocks had to be conserved. The School almost ran out several times and each delivery was greeted with profound relief. At different times in 1982 there were bus and rail strikes which affected school attendance. In May 1984 the teaching unions took prolonged action over various issues relating to pay and conditions of service. Some areas of the country were harder hit than others but the greatest disruption occurred in the secondary sector. At the Grammar School action was usually limited to single days or parts of days by individual unions. Further disruption was caused when unions nationally and locally instructed members not to cover for absent colleagues and not to undertake a variety of activities, including supervision at lunchtime. This meant that pupils could remain in school only to eat their meal. There were times when, because of a lack of covering staff, lessons were cancelled and pupils had a late start or were sent home early. Some Parents' Evenings had to be cancelled. Some pupil reports were sent home with a grade but no teacher comment. Schools in the early eighties were not always happy places and there is no doubt that there were tensions both within schools and between schools and the wider community. Not all teachers agreed with the union action. Those who did, felt they were acting to defend not only their professional status but the quality of the education service. Many parents, inevitably, viewed the situation as it affected their children and some were angry at what was happening. Normal service was eventually resumed in June 1986, but the 'action' had gone on for two years and it took some time before the old trust was re-established.

But it wasn't all doom and gloom. Schools continued to work successfully during these years. It was clearly stated by teachers that the union action should not interfere with preparation for examinations and indeed the Grammar School's results continued to improve throughout the 1980s. The main representative sports teams were still hockey and netball for girls and rugby and cricket for boys, though soccer was increasing in popularity and the focus for cricket, especially at senior level, was becoming local clubs rather than schools. Other games were coming to the fore and there were local leagues for most of them. Tennis was already well-established, basketball and volleyball teams competed regularly and in 1985 the Senior Girls, Senior Boys and Senior Mixed badminton teams all won their leagues. Money was raised for good causes; an ingenious array of activities including a squash marathon, sponsored bunny hops and the first non-uniform day, with some teachers appearing in alarming costumes ranging from a German officer to full hunting gear, raised £3,000 for the Ethiopian Famine Relief Fund. Two teachers, David Eldridge and Nigel Helliwell cycled from Lands End to John o'Groats for cancer research and school funds. Pupils worked with local charities, Help the Aged and Ilkley Good Neighbours. There was the ironically-titled 'Soft Option' exhibition of Art work at the Manor House, of which the Gazette said, "School shows tend to attract a slightly patronising attitude. Not this one." For the first time, meetings were held to give parents and pupils information about fourth- and fifth-year courses. BTEC students compiled a video about controversial proposed cuts to the Ilkley rail service, including an interview with local MP Gary Waller. The Head of Physical Science, Andrew Lambert, was one of only five teachers in the country to receive the Institute of Physics Award for "outstanding teaching." The Parents' Association began to produce a regular newsletter and in 1986 became a Parent-Teacher Association. One of its first projects was to raise almost £4,000 to replace the hall and stage curtains.

At 16-plus pupils took either the GCE, which had operated since 1951 or the newer Certificate of Secondary Education. It was a clumsy and divisive duality and it was no surprise when the two were amalgamated as the GCSE in 1986. There was the inevitable dispute over resources, with teachers throughout the country complaining that the change had not been properly

Nigel Duce conducts the School Orchestra in 1982.

funded. The Governors complained to Sir Keith Joseph, the Education Minister and had a meeting with Gary Waller. Some extra money was eventually forthcoming and, for the first time, the government decreed that two training days should be set aside to allow teachers to prepare. Meanwhile Bradford Local Authority was divided into six consortia, with upper schools and local colleges encouraged to provide joint courses. Ilkley's distance from its linked areas of Keighley and Bingley made provision difficult but nevertheless the School was able to develop post-16 vocational courses with Bradford and Keighley Colleges. It worked with Ilkley College on a Unified Vocational Project, which was designed to bridge the gap between school and employment. A Work Practice Unit, designed to serve consortium schools and based at Keighley, was opened by Sir John Harvey-Jones. An innovative course, based on the new electronic office environment and developed in conjunction with the Dutch town of Arnhem, was piloted at Ilkley in 1987. The government's first sortie into major curriculum development, the Technical and Vocational Education Initiative was funded to the tune of £7m in Bradford LEA. For the first time the School was able to appoint a full-time chartered librarian, Kathy Fuller. New subjects such as Computer Studies and Sociology made their appearance. The receipt of ten Nimbus computers ensured the provision of a GCSE Computer Studies course.

Many out-of-school activities continued throughout the union 'action' and the range expanded once it was over. There were annual 'A' level Fieldwork visits, Geography to Bamburgh, History and Sociology to London and Science to Sellafield. There was a School Expedition to Iceland in 1983, when, as Will Varley recalls, "the 24 expedition members spent summer in Iceland, camping in the remote interior, visiting geysers, volcanoes and spectacular waterfalls and climbing the highest peak on the island, Hvannadalshnukur." There was an Outdoor Activities Week for 100 pupils and staff based at Rosthwaite in the Lake District, a forerunner of what were to become annual Residential Weeks in the Dales. The musical 'Cabaret' was produced by Sue Garnett. Business Studies students opened a bookshop at Ilkley Middle School. An exhibition of the School's Art work, 'Where's the Green?' at the Manor House attracted around 3,000 visitors. Each October a year group of over 200 pupils did two weeks' work experience. A sixth former, Kathryn Shann, won a top national award in the Schools Design Prize Competition. She designed a musical activity centre for pre-school special care children and was presented with her award by the Secretary of State for Education, John MacGregor. In 1983 for the first time all three local candidates in the General Election went head to head in front of a packed school hall. Events such as the Careers and Higher Education Conventions, the Open Evening, Comic Relief

July 1984 - Six teachers look forward to retirement.

Back row: Ruth Hill, Des Birch, Maeve Hyndman.

Front row: Jim Bailey, Madge Pearson, Eric Whitaker.

Between them they had given 134 years' service to the School.

Day, the annual School Quiz set by David Kilvington for Cancer Research and the Carol Service organised by Nigel Duce at the Priory Church at Bolton Abbey became regular features of the school year. The Sixth Form Christmas Party was always a colourful affair. Margaret Chambers remembers one around 1984 when another teacher, Robert Haigh, arrived dressed as a punk. "He had bright green hair and face and was swathed in chains he had borrowed from the caretaker, Bill Aveyard. The sixth formers didn't recognise him – nor did his own little boy."

There were significant staff changes, none more so than in 1984 when both Madge Pearson, Deputy Head, and Eric Whitaker, Head of Sixth Form, retired. In 1986 Clive Allen, who had been a Deputy Head for almost ten years, moved on. Two years later his successor, David Simpson, and two others were killed by a rockfall in a cave at Ease Gill near Kirkby Lonsdale. In his short time at Ilkley David had impressed greatly. At a simple ceremony on the school lawn a tree was planted in his memory by his widow. He was succeeded by Ian Gasper, who remained in the post until 2006. At the same time news came of the death of Mr Sparham who had been Senior Science Master from 1930 until his retirement in 1954. Other long-serving staff retired – Gordon McLachlan, who had helped plant the Coronation Pole thirty years earlier, Jean Edwards and Ruth Hill from the P.E. Department, Mike Selina from History, Maeve Hyndman from Home Economics, and Jim Bailey, who had taught at both the Secondary and Grammar Schools. In retrospect it can be seen as another of those balancing points between past and future for, as the School bade farewell to those who had played such an important role in its past, a new educational landscape was already appearing on the horizon. Soon there would be major developments of such importance that they continue to influence the way schools work today.

Deputy Head David Simpson, who died in a potholing accident in 1988.

Judith Leach

The New Order

The Conservative Government began seriously to address educational issues in the second half of the 1980s. Many of the questions they chose to confront had been flagged by James Callaghan in 1976 and had been an underlying theme in educational debate in the ensuing ten years. In particular, issues such as what schools taught, how their success could be measured and to whom they were accountable were now seen as the legitimate concern of central government and an Education Act in 1986 began to address them. In response to the various disputes about hours and duties, the government put a figure on the amount of 'directed' time a teacher should work annually – 1265 hours – and, from 1987, heads had to produce time budgets for contractual activities. An annual report to parents on the life and work of a school now had to be published and a meeting held at which it could be discussed. Ilkley's experience was not untypical: the Head, senior staff and governors lined up for the first such meeting in 1987 not quite knowing what to expect. The outcome, then and in future years, turned out to be an amiable evening attended by a handful of parents. The Act also led to adjustments to the Governing Body; henceforth there would be two Teacher Governors, two Parent Governors and, in a short-lived experiment, a Pupil Governor.

Peter Wood, Headteacher 1979 - 2002.

The Education Reform Act of 1988 was a different animal altogether. It re-ordered the educational landscape in a way which affected every school in the country. It established a National Curriculum, which specified what should be taught, and Key Stages, at the end of which pupils would be tested on what they had learned. Henceforth the exam results of all schools would be published. It provided for the Local Management of Schools, whereby budgetary control would be removed from local authorities and given to heads and governors. It introduced the concept of grant maintained status, which enabled schools, after a ballot of parents, to remove themselves from local authorities and be funded by central government. It required that all pupils "on each school day take part in an act of collective worship which shall be wholly or mainly of a broadly Christian character." Thus it was a curious amalgam of central direction and delegation and it was soon to be underpinned by the establishment of the Office for Standards in Education (Ofsted).

The National Curriculum sought to give every child a broad and balanced education. As well as stipulating what should be taught, it indicated what proportion of the week should be devoted to each curriculum area. This meant not only developing new courses but having to shoe-horn subjects into a congested timetable. In response to the pressures being heaped on teachers, five days each year were to be set aside for training, known universally as 'Baker Days' after the then Education Minister. Fortunately the introduction of the National Curriculum in secondary schools was phased over two years, as were the Local Management regulations. At first only the minor budget headings were delegated but by 1991, with the inclusion of staffing, the Grammar School Governors suddenly found themselves responsible for an annual budget of almost £2m. This all placed great pressure on governing bodies. Ilkley, with a supportive community able to offer a wide range of skills, was fortunate; it was not so in all schools. The role of governor became a major undertaking. The School's Governing Body met twice-termly, as did its five committees. Each governor sat on two of these, needed to be available for appointment interviews and was generally expected to lend support at a variety of functions and meetings during the year. As with the Head and Staff, the Governing Body was subject to inspection by Ofsted. It was a demanding schedule for what was an unpaid job usually done by busy people.

The establishment of Key Stages with end-of-stage tests was seen as largely irrelevant, partly because the tests were voluntary to begin with (the School did not complete its first tests until 1993) and partly because in any case the key stage boundaries did not coincide with the ages of transfer in a three-tier system. The new nomenclature, in which year groups were numbered sequentially, felt very awkward at first; for many teachers and parents Year Nine would always be the Third Year and they couldn't even bear to think of the Sixth Form as Years Twelve and Thirteen.

The provision for grant maintained schools was difficult to ignore, especially as governors were obliged to consider it annually and report that they had done so. Levels of funding in Bradford schools were depressingly low and by 1992 four upper schools had already taken the decision to 'opt out'. In that year the Ilkley Governors, chaired by John Sanders, bit the bullet and decided to ballot parents. The essence of the debate was financial. A grant maintained school had a significantly greater amount of funding delegated, mainly for services normally provided by the Local Authority. It could then decide how to use this money. The Governors published figures which demonstrated that the School could be up to £200,000 a year better off if it opted out. The Director of Education, not surprisingly, disputed this and pointed out that, if some schools opted out of central provision, those remaining would suffer a diminished service. There were meetings in the King's Hall and at the School. The Ilkley Gazette ran articles 'For' and 'Against' and for two months the debate raged. In December 1992 63% of the parents voted against the proposals and the matter was over as quickly as it had begun. Indeed the tide had already turned. The number of schools opting out was declining and, although they undoubtedly benefited in the interim, by 1998 all grant maintained schools were returned to local authorities.

The publication of exam results marked a significant shift of policy for the School. Hitherto individual results had always been regarded as the personal property of the student. Heads gave governors the overall statistics each year but, because there was no consistent framework, it was difficult to make comparisons. In 1991 the Sunday Times broke new ground by asking schools to send in their A Level results according to a template. When they were published in September, Ilkley Grammar found itself in a national list of the Top 20 state schools. As every paper began to publish 'league tables' in the immediate aftermath of results days each August, and the government produced its own statistics each November, the School continued, and continues still, to rate among the top comprehensives in the country.

These years represented a time of enormous national change and it is impossible to divorce developments at Ilkley from the wider context. Yet much that was taking place had nothing to do with these great affairs of state but was simply about the School continuing to extend its provision. A paragraph from the Head's Report to Parents for 1989 gives some indication of the kind activities that were going on:

There have been several foreign visits: a sixth form visit to Russia, a ski trip to Austria, participation in the Yorkshire-

...T TIMES - 8 SEPTEMBER 1991

250 OF THE BEST

FOCUS

T&A, Tuesday, September 10, 1991

'Tremendous boost' as results announced

School joins A-level top 20

School success in exam league

A-level performance across the country

ILKLEY Grammar School is one of the top three mixed comprehensive schools in England and Wales it was revealed this week.

In a special A level results survey, based upon A and B grades, carried out by a national newspaper, Ilkley Grammar was ranked in the top 20 secondary schools.

Of the 4,200 secondary schools in England and Wales, just two other comprehensive schools finished with a higher percentage of A and B grades.

The findings delighted Ilkley Grammar headmaster, Mr Wood who said:

"This comes as a tremendous boost for [they] are very responsible. They work very hard [and experi]ence and well[behaved pu]pils."

By CHRIS DAGGETT

out the school so the pupils know what is expected of them and what they should be aiming for. There is an excellent tutorial system in which students are seen as individuals and their progress is monitored and advice given. All these factors have made a contribution to our success and not just at A level.

"I am not surprised by the results," said Mr Wood, "we have had excellent results for many years now.

"Obviously I am delighted we have come so high and finished as the county's top ranked school."

But Mr Wood keen to point out the examinations are the be-all and end

of education. "There are many other things which come together to make a good school. What we are striving to do is produce well-rounded students," he commented.

The two comprehensive schools that finished above Ilkley Grammar were King David Hebrew, Liverpool and Llanharry Welsh Language, Wales.

A WEST Yorkshire school has been named as one of Britain's top 20 state schools for A-level results.

Ilkley Grammar came joint 18th position in [a] Sunday newspaper survey which showed [that] out of the school's A-level pupils, 48 per cent [score]d A and B

West Yorkshire's Prince [Henry's] Grammar, [came] in joint [18th] with 38 per [cent results at the] two grades.

Both schools — despite their "grammar" titles — are comprehensive and have no selection procedure.

Their placings put them ahead of hundreds of grammar schools which select their pupils by testing.

DELIGHT

They are also ahead of many fee-paying independent schools.

Ilkley Grammar head Mr Peter Wood said: "We are one of only three comprehensive schools in the top 20 so we are delighted.

"We have have an experienced and hard working staff and some excellent students.

"The teachers' experience enables them to point out to students what is expected from them and what they should be aiming for.

"We encourage self-reliance and self-motivation and don't spoon-feed our pupils."

Mr Wood said the school historically did well in exams.

ILKLEY Grammar School was celebrating today after being placed high in a league table of A Level results from schools across the UK.

The survey of 250 of the country's top schools has listed Ilkley as joint 18th with some of the highest grades in Britain.

Nearly half the pupils who took the exams this year scored with either A or B grades, and the school in Cowpasture Road, Ilkley, was one of only three comprehensives to appear in the first twenty.

Headmaster Peter Wood paid tribute to the staff and pupils for their commitment to the school.

"It is marvellous [that our] students who are [to] put in the work [make the] most of their [talents,] the results are [so hi]gh [that they] deserved," he [said].

"...obvious for every...to have it...they are...best in the...absolutely

"School in [Ilk]ley, was [a Sunday] survey, [48 per] cent of [whom got] A or [B grades.]

TOP 250

(school listing table, mostly illegible)

School | | |
Haberdashers' Aske's Elstree... | |
King David Hebrew, Liverpool | |
Keswick School, Reading | |
Royal Grammar, High Wycombe | |
Wycombe High | |
Dr Challoner's High, Bucks | |
Hills Road, Cambridge | |
Llanharry Welsh Language, Wales | |
King Edward VI, Chelmsford | |
Colchester Royal, Essex | |
Watford Boys, Herts | |
Tunbridge Wells Girls, Kent | |
Colchester County High, Essex | |
Lancaster Royal, Lancs | |
Tiffin Girls, Kingston-upon-Thames | |
Tiffin Boys, Kingston, Bucks | |
Dr Challoner's Grammar, Bucks | |
Old Swinford Hospital, Stourbridge | |
Ilkley Grammar, Yorks | |
Chelmsford County High, Essex | |
Ysgol Tryfan bilingual, Bangor | |
Latymer, Edmonton, London | |
St Bernard's convent, Slough | |
St Bernard West, Orpington | |
Newstead Wood, Orpington | |
The Clarendon School, Oxford | |
St David's, Orpington | |
Wallington High, Wallington | |
Barking Abbey, Essex | |
Kenilworth School, Kenilworth | |
Langley Grammar, Slough | |
Wycliffe Wells School, Aberdare | |
Aberdare Boys School, Aberdare | |
Sir William Borlase's, Bucks | |
Kings School, Peterborough | |
The Kings School, Grantham | |
Northampton College, Merton | |
Pimlico School, London | |
Colston Grammar School, Devon | |
Bishopshalt, Hillingdon | |
Bishop Cotts High, Swansea | |
Ilford County High, Essex | |
Gunsford County, Surrey | |
Wolverhampton High, West Midlands | |
Aylesbury High, Bucks | |
South Park, Middlesbrough | |
Verdin High, Ulverston | |

Westphalia exchange, an exchange visit with a school in Berlin, a third year visit to Coutainville and the 1989 Coutances exchange visit which this year was massively over-subscribed. Nearer to home activities included History and Sociology residentials in London, a Geography field course in Northumberland, a Physical Science course in Cumbria, a languages course at Lancaster University, a fifth year Outdoor Activities Day at Buckden, a weekend at Wimbledon and numerous theatre visits. The third, fourth and sixth years enjoyed an Activities Day in July. A four day Induction Course was organised for 135 new sixth form students. The Art Exhibition at the Manor House attracted hundreds of visitors over three weeks. There was a one-day Higher Education Convention and a subsequent Careers Convention, both with many exhibitors and customers. Links with local industries have continued to develop, particularly through programmes of visits and work experience. Charity work includes support for Oxfam, the Armenian Earthquake Disaster Fund, The Hillsborough Disaster Fund and Comic Relief, for which the fifth year alone raised over £1,000. School teams and individual pupils gained success in hockey, soccer, badminton, cross-country, athletics and tennis, with less traditional sports such as ten-pin bowling and girls' soccer proving popular.

By 1989 computer cabling had been installed for a network covering most of the main building. Henceforth access was available from seventy points and all pupils were registered as users and had their own passwords. Later in the year a computerised administration network was fitted and gradually more areas were able to benefit from the new technology, not least the Library, where the power of the new internet was greeted with a mixture of marvel and disbelief. Inevitably the financial position constrained the School's ability to exploit the new technology, but it was able to update its networks and supplement its budgetary provision with assistance from the PTA and by collecting thousands of Tesco vouchers each year.

The government was aware that, although exam results were critical in judging the success of a school, many other elements went into the mix. Accordingly in the early 1990s it began to

Opposite page:

The publication of A level exam results by the Sunday Times in 1991 led to an explosion of interest in 'league tables' and, incidentally, a lot of publicity for the School.

develop, with Her Majesty's Inspectorate and under the new Ofsted umbrella, a system for regular inspection. Previous inspections, under HMI, had been pretty relaxed and infrequent affairs. Now things would be different. Schools would need to provide a blizzard of statistics. Not only would governors be involved, but parents would be sent questionnaires, invited to a meeting and asked to comment on a school. Inspection Reports would be available as quickly as possible, a longer version for the school and a shorter version for parents. Details would be published in the press — and soon on the internet. Several schools were required to trial the arrangements. Ilkley Grammar School received the glad tidings in March 1993 that it was to be one of them.

The resulting report, fifteen years on, now has the status of a historical document and it certainly presented the most detailed picture of the school to date. In its eighty four paragraphs it analysed Standards and Quality, Efficiency, The School as a Community and Subjects of the Curriculum (minus, curiously, History, P.E. and all the Creative Arts). If the School was apprehensive before the event, it was certainly reassured afterwards by the 'Main Findings', even allowing for the curiously stilted Ofsted style:

The first Year 11 May Ball was organised by the Parent Teacher Association in 1990. It has since become a regular annual event. Pictured here are revellers from the 1991 Ball, held at the Craiglands.

This is a very good school. Standards of achievement are good and at times outstanding. Examination results at GCSE and A Level are well above national averages. The quality of teaching and learning is good. Expectations are high, the pace of lessons is brisk and pupils are challenged to think rigorously. Pupils respond well. They are confident and conscientious and participate enthusiastically in lessons. The behaviour of pupils is excellent. Relationships between staff and pupils and amongst pupils are good. The school's leadership has succeeded in creating an environment where good standards of work and teaching and learning of high quality are achieved.

The tone of such comments now is relatively commonplace, as all schools are regularly inspected. In 1993 they were very new and excited a lot of curiosity and publicity. They also gave the School confidence in addressing the major issues it faced.

None of these was greater than the budget. There had been

A pair of clowns from one of the first three-legged fancy-dress 'walks' round the town in aid of Children in Need. They began in the early 1990s and continue to be an annual event.

hopes that the delegation of funding would mean more prosperous times. The reality proved different. For a few years there was a small surplus which was prudently put by for a rainy day. In 1992 the deluge arrived. The Ofsted report set it out clearly: "In the present financial year approximately £100,000 has been used from last year's contingency funds to maintain the current standards of provision." So it was that in one year the reserves were gone. Thereafter the situation simply got worse. For some reason Bradford schools seemed to be among the worst funded in the country. Heads and Governors lobbied Councillors, MPs, the Director of Education – anyone who would listen, but it made no difference. Bradford (Labour) said the Government (Conservative) wasn't giving it enough money. The Government said it had increased the amount made available and Bradford should review its priorities. Perhaps the truth lay somewhere between. Education funding remained an impenetrable mystery; it was said at the time that three people had once understood it but two died and the third went mad. The result was that over half the upper schools in the Bradford Authority were running deficit budgets by the mid 1990s, some quite astronomically. Heads lobbied and protested; one even turning up for a photo opportunity outside City Hall with a cape and rapier to illustrate the 'cuts'. The Governors made all reasonable economies but drew the line at a crude removal of subjects from the curriculum or at class sizes over thirty. The Head's Report to Governors in May 1996 shows how bad the situation had become:

> In 1989, when Local Management was introduced, this school had 924 pupils and 67 teachers. In 1996-7 we anticipate 1055 pupils and a teaching staff of 58. Throughout this time the School has striven to maintain its standards, exam results have improved and we continue to be over-subscribed. If we were in any of our neighbouring local authorities it is no exaggeration to say we would be hundreds of thousands of pounds better off. As it is, we have to believe either that the government discriminates against Bradford or that Bradford simply does not organise its finances effectively.

An important means of relaying this and other aspects of school life to parents and the community was the Newsletter, first published in February 1992. One of the teachers, Byron Bradley, was involved in an exchange with a school in Perth, Western Australia, and returned from his year away having picked up the idea of a regular newsletter. He was its first editor, it has since gone through hundreds of editions and it is still going strong. It

*The first edition
of the School
Newsletter.
Much improved
and after
several hundred
editions, it
remains an
important link
with parents
and the
community.*

ILKLEY GRAMMAR SCHOOL NEWSLETTER

February 1992   No. 1

INTRODUCTION

This is the first edition of what we intend will be a monthly newsletter to parents. It will take the place of the multitude of letters and notices the school produces which sometimes reach home but which at times progress no further than the bottom of a bag or pocket. It will be published on the last Friday of each month. If you do not receive it then you can demand it, confident that it will have been given to your son or daughter that day. In order to confirm that the system is working, we are including with the first two issues a reply slip, on the back page of the newsletter. I should be grateful if you would complete this and return it to your son's or daughter's group tutor by Friday, 7th February.

Inevitably we shall have to be selective in what we include but we shall attempt to give you information about the most important aspects of school life. There will be reports from staff, governors, pupils and parents. There will be news of forthcoming events and information about school, Local Authority and Government policies which will affect your children. I hope it will become a very important element in the growing partnership between school and parents.

Peter Wood.

BUCKDEN RESIDENTIAL

Buckden ! A name to strike terror in the hearts of some, but hopefully, not too many in Year 9. 160 pupils and 21 staff took part in the two-week rolling programme at the outdoor centre.

New skills and thrills were experienced as all took part in, amongst other things, caving, walking, abseiling and the zip-wire. The Task Day found teams finding new ways of crossing a river (or falling in!) Signs of our presence will be found in a wood as some pupils spent time cutting down trees as part of a conservation programme run by the National Park Warden.

Of particular interest to parents are the other skills acquired; gravy making, mashing potatoes, laying tables and washing up. I should give cocoa a miss !

Making beds is no longer a mystery! Did you know there are 160 ways to put on a duvet cover?

Early signs suggest a lot of fun was shared by pupils and staff, the latter are still smiling.

We hope to have a video and photographs on display at the Year 9 Parents' Evenings.

was sometimes the less obvious pieces that caught the eye; these from the first edition:

Lost Property: By half term the office had collected 14 school sweaters, 4 games kits, 5 jackets, a completed cookery project, several keys and five pairs of glasses.

Children in Need: Mr Beaumont has agreed to support this year's Children in Need appeal by shaving off his beard – half at a time. However he is only prepared to do this if £100 is raised.

Accounts of the Year 9 Residentials were always good value, whether from pupils (Jessie Pemberton and Jenny Coleman):

The weather was fairly dismal when we arrived. What we didn't know was that this was as good as it was going to get. On the first night we did country dancing while the other half went night orienteering in howling gales or horizontal rain.

or a teacher (Ian Swain):

My memorable moments include the look on pupils' faces as one of the instructors was telling them he once knew a horse that drank eight buckets full of beer each Saturday night and then couldn't stand up on Sunday morning, and seeing Claire, when climbing Strans Gill, stopping in mid-stream with water pouring over her head, down her waterproofs and out through her trouser legs.

Departmental needs could be unusual:

If you are a keen fisherman, could you spare a few maggots to feed Sally the Salamander in the Biology Department? A fortnightly donation of ten wiggly maggots would be wonderful.

So could Comic Relief stunts:

One 175 foot crane, an extremely long piece of elastic, £200 for charity and a 100% adrenaline rush later Kathryn and Michael Wheatley landed safely on planet Earth only to find their heads were still in the clouds. Or, if you have no faith in rubber bands, then follow in the footsteps of daredevils Kate Storey and Tom Griffin by abseiling down off the

Staff celebrate a 'sponsored slim' in 1992.

L to R: Jean Williams, Barbara Greathead, Charlotte Hopton, Linda Curran, Joan Prout, Sylvia Noble, Nicola Vernon, Maureen Shackleton and Janet Wilson, together with their trainer.

Peter Wood receives the first minibus donated by the Parent Teacher Association from PTA Chair Janet Munro in July 1992.

School's roof. These sixth formers' skills and ropes and ouch . . . harnesses earned them much kudos and Comic Relief a lot of money.

The budget situation meant the School needed all the financial help it could get. The Parent Teacher Association hit a rich vein when they discovered the popularity of car boot sales on the field on a Sunday morning. From small beginnings these developed into enormous affairs organised with military precision. Before long it was not uncommon, given a fine morning, for one sale to yield four figure profits. Whereas traditionally PTA money had funded 'extras' – and it continued to do so, most notably two mini-buses – it was now required to augment mainstream spending. The Friends of Ilkley Grammar School, comprising representatives of School and community, developed a covenanting scheme and by 1998 had donated over £20,000 to key projects. Neither was sufficient to compensate for inadequate central funding but both made a difference to what could be afforded.

In 1993 the School celebrated a hundred years at Cowpasture Road. There was a real sense of history about the occasion and, as publicity spread, former pupils, some going as far back as Atkinson days, made contact and even donated memorabilia. Tony Barringer wrote his book of 'Recollections'. Elizabeth Howard organised an exhibition drawn from the archive. There was a Thanksgiving Service in St Margaret's Church (whither Mr Atkinson had led the boys to their Sunday worship eighty years earlier) at which the speaker was Mr Hughes. The Head wrote:

> In spite of the incremental pace of change of the past hundred years, there are many things Mr Swann, my predecessor of 1893, would recognise today – some of the buildings, the school crest, elements of the curriculum and most of all the interaction of teaching and learning which lies at the heart of a school.

In 1990 Jack Layfield died. He had been a governor for many years, including a period as Chairman. He was a good friend to the School and, even when his health began to fail, was keen to remain involved. In January 1994 Marjorie Jackman and Barbara Cussons retired from the Governing Body. Both had given many years of service and each had a long association with the School. Marjorie Jackman had been a pupil from 1940-47. She was elected President of the Old Olicanians' Association in 1963 and in 1964 became the first former pupil to be appointed as a governor. Subsequently her children and grandchildren were pupils. Barbara Cussons' family connections began with her father, whom she

ILKLEY GRAMMAR SCHOOL
1893 - 1993
CENTENARY EVENTS

TO COMMEMORATE ONE HUNDRED YEARS ON THE PRESENT SCHOOL SITE

MONDAY 20 SEPTEMBER

EXHIBITION OF PHOTOGRAPHS AND MEMORABILIA
School Library, 2.45 - 5.00 p.m.

**PUBLICATION OF "ILKLEY GRAMMAR SCHOOL -
A CENTURY AT SCHOOL, 1893 - 1993"** by A. F. Barringer.
On sale at the school.

FRIDAY 24 SEPTEMBER

EXHIBITION As above

SERVICE OF THANKSGIVING
St. Margaret's Church, Ilkley 7.00p.m.
Address given by Mr. R. Hughes, Headmaster, 1970 - 1979

**INFORMAL GATHERING OF PAST AND PRESENT PUPILS,
STAFF AND FRIENDS OF THE SCHOOL,
AND LAUNCH OF P.T.A. CENTENARY MINIBUS APPEAL.**
At school, 8.00 - 10.00 p.m.

Exhibition may be viewed at other times until Tuesday, 12 October, by prior appointment.
Some items will be on display at the School's Open Evening on Wednesday, 13 October.
FOR DETAILS, TELEPHONE SCHOOL OFFICE, ILKLEY 608424

September 1993 - the 100th anniversary of the Cowpasture Road building. Pupils Rifhat Awan, Alan McCulloch, David Bacher and Tracy Smith dust down an old book and look into the School's history.

Ilkley Gazette.

183

followed as a pupil in 1943. She was elected to the Governing Body in 1979 as a representative of the Parish Council. The Newsletter also carried occasional tidings of former pupils; in 1994 Michael Turnbull (1944-53) became Bishop of Durham and in the same year Anna Dixon (1985-90) was President of the Cambridge University Union. The usual round of staff changes was recorded, none more notably than the retirement in 1997 of Ivan Minto, who had been appointed Head of Art and Creative Studies in 1971 and had been Head of Sixth Form since 1986. There was no mistaking the affection with which he was regarded by sixth formers: "His broad minded and unusual affinity for teenagers meant all voices could be heard. Thank you, respect and best wishes from all your loyal Mintonians, past and present. (Souvenir bow ties available in memory of a great era.)"

The re-introduction in 1990 of Speech Day at the King's Hall gave an opportunity for public recognition of achievement. By 1995 this had developed into less formal Presentation Evenings where, at two separate events at the Craiglands, exam certificates were presented and speeches were kept to a minimum. The same venue also witnessed for the first time in 1990 the Year Eleven May Ball where, with the help of gowns and tuxedos, pupils were transformed into society sophisticates, arriving in every form of transport from stretch limos to tractors. Another annual event developed at this time was the Year Nine Residential when, for a week, new pupils lived together at Ingleborough Hall or Buckden House and had to manage such challenges as potholes, rope bridges and stream walking. The opportunity of two weeks' Work Experience was extended to every Year Ten pupil, some finding quite exotic placements. Plays were produced each year, some the high-profile 'School Play' ('The Caucasian Chalk Circle', 'The Little Shop of Horrors') as well as others produced (and in some cases written) by sixth formers with a cast of younger pupils. In a bizarre but predictably popular event, Year Nine began to raise money for Children in Need by an annual three-legged fancy dress walk round the town.

The building was now showing its age. When a Victorian ceiling collapsed at Bingley Grammar School in 1988, it was decreed that all lath and plaster work at Ilkley should be replaced. Sections of the old building were closed and scaffolding sprouted overnight, a situation not helped when asbestos was discovered in parts of the roof. Providentially, this work and the subsequent re-wiring and redecoration meant that

The Rt. Revd. Michael Turnbull, an Old Olicanian, became Bishop of Durham in 1994.

Picture by courtesy of Michael Turnbull and the Bishop's Secretary.

Majorie Jackman and Barbara Cussons retire from the Governing Body in January 1994.

Philip Bainbridge.

when, under Local Management, the building was handed over to the Governors, it was in reasonably good order. But it was becoming clear that it was not big enough. By 1992 numbers had increased to the point where there simply weren't enough rooms. Not only the accommodation but the intake now needed to be managed. John Cockshott, the new Chairman of Governors, reported to parents the following year on the steps taken:

> The School's academic success was becoming better and better known and more parents wished to send their children here as a result. We were seeing our resources – particularly accommodation – overstretched by the increase in intake. The intake is governed by the 'Standard Admission Number'. To preserve the overall quality of education we decided with considerable reluctance that we needed to reduce the Standard Number from 287 to 247.

This, and the provision of four temporary rooms, gave some breathing space and meant all children from the three middle schools could be accommodated. But overcrowding remained, particularly in specialist areas such as Science. The local press had a field day, making all sorts of imaginative suggestions as to where the School might re-locate, from the Scalebor Park site to

The Year 9 Residentials at Buckden House and Ingleborough Hall began in the late 1980s.

Andrew Lambert helped to organise the activities and took many photos, which were later donated to the School by his family.

Ilkley College. At the urgent request of the Ilkley Pyramid, the Local Authority launched a 'Wharfe Valley Review' to look at how best pupil numbers from five to eighteen could be managed at a time of population growth. The report, published in 1995, was a major disappointment, containing little more than an outline of the current position and some statistics.

By now there was an annual Open Evening. This was a major event at which huge numbers of parents and children toured the building and saw pupils working. An impressive brochure was produced, which detailed the organisation and curriculum. The 1996 edition gave a typical outline:

> On entry into Year Nine, pupils are placed in a mixed ability tutor group. The group tutor, where possible, remains with the group throughout the three years in main school. Pupils are registered in these groups and have one tutorial period each week with their tutor. For academic teaching, pupils are grouped according to their general ability on the recommendation of Middle Schools.

All pupils in Year Nine followed a common curriculum based on a government template. The National Curriculum then determined the organisation of 'core' and 'compulsory' subjects in Years Ten and Eleven. The core was Maths, English, Science, Design Technology, P.E. and Games, and Social, Personal and Careers Education. The optional element comprised one Modern Language

The Upper Sixth - May 1994

Back row: Ben Bridgen, Nick Beanland, Chris Walsh, Matthew Steer, Ruth Lambert, Richard Wood, Andrew Thornley, Ch.

Fourth row: Matthew Sinker, Jamie Allen, Matthew Hodgson, Martin Waite, Matthew Papper, Carl Groth, Iain Lumsden, Ju
Libby Wells, Jill Brown, Liz Rowan, Sarah Thorpe, Kirsten Mason.

Third row: Lucy Warwick, Ben Button, Daniel Penn, Matthew Harvey, Andrew Gregory, Katie Moon, Ben Whittaker, Cla
Clare Pennock, Helen Cartright, Lucy Bullen, Helen Ellington, Clare Foreman, Jo Railton, Lucinda Warnes.

*Second row: Victoria Jones, Vicki Timmons, Johanna Hoyal, Helen Etchell, Caroline Howard, Katie Turner, **David Bullock***
Wasser, Helen Sowman, Shogo Suzuki, Simon Pitt, Simon Farrand.

Front row: Tim Parry, Michelle Anderson, Vicky Sheldon, Clare Green, Rachel Exley, Melanie Kingston, Lola Smith, Jaq
Jo Thornhill, Emma Uden, Sonia Coulton, Beverley Phillips, Elinor McKeown, Emma Kershaw, David Rayner, Leah Gibso

en, Alex Pickard, Chris Watson, Dan Hawksley, James White, Daniel Fitch, Chris Keeling, James Sayers, Bobby Diggles.

Camilla Frankis, Carol Mason, Katherine Harris, Judith Eldridge, Kuljit Jagpal, Ruth Shann, Neil Goodwin, Erika Evans,

apman, Sally Boyle, Emily Whelan, Emma Sunderland, Charlotte Parker, Lucy Howard, Catherine Elder, Hannah Wells,

drew Lambert, Chris Stockums, Ivan Minto, Glen Nothers, John Wright (staff), *Ruth Stewart, Daniel Laughey, Sarah*

dd, Hannah Gill, Kathy Sharp, Jacky Mills, Teresa McDonnel, Jenny Duttine, Carthiga Senathirajah, Victoria Munro, ie Hill.

The Under 15 Hockey Team - Champions of Bradford and West Yorkshire 1995.

Back row: Tessa Hutchinson, Stevie Upton, Ann Newman, Rosalind Gooch, Beth Kyle, Abigale Farrant, Judith Lee.
Front row: Katie Appleyard, Rosie Townsley, Emma Tweddle, Lousie Dobson, Catherine Brown, Tara Booluck.

The 1997 Election with candidates Emma Tweddle, Mark Roberts, Peter Scott, Steven Bradbury, Andrew Pollard and Sam Pick.

Ilkley Gazette.

(from French, German and Spanish), one Humanity (from History, Geography, Economics and Religious Education) and an 'open' option (from a second Language or Humanity, Art, Music, Drama or Home Economics). There was much more freedom in the Sixth Form, where students could chose from an impressive list of eighteen 'A' Levels as well as a one-year or two-year GNVQ course in Business and Finance or a two-year BTEC course in Health Studies.

In 1997 Ofsted returned. In those days schools were given lots of time to prepare, so it was known as early as May 1996 that there would be an inspection in February 1997. The intention was to be helpful; the effect was to raise anxiety levels. In the event all was well:

> Ilkley Grammar School is a very good school. It provides a high quality of education which enables pupils to reach high standards of attainment and to develop their personal skills and qualities. Pupils benefit from a positive ethos, a good quality of support and guidance and from the strong partnership the school enjoys with parents and the community. Behaviour is good and pupils show remarkable self-discipline as they move around restricted corridors between lessons. With appropriate and good-humoured support from teachers, pupils in all year groups respond well to high expectations and to the intellectual demands made on them.

> The Headteacher offers strong and decisive leadership which is delivered with conviction and integrity. He is well supported by a hard working and committed senior management team and together they give a clear direction to the work of the School. The Governing Body works hard and provides a secure framework within which policies are devised, good practice is developed and the School is organised and managed.

As a summary of progress and achievement during a time of immense change, it was reassuring. It might even have been thought that the report heralded a quieter, more settled period, as the major reforms of the past ten years bedded in. What nobody quite realised was that nothing could have been further from the truth.

Back To The Future

The three-tier system had worked well in the Ilkley Pyramid for almost thirty years. Indeed it was viewed as a strength. The schools were seen to be successful. Each community, Addingham, Ilkley and Burley, cherished and was proud of its local first and middle schools. The close liaison between the phases led to a continuity which was valued by teachers and parents alike. The educational experience of the Pyramid was deliberately marketed as a linked and carefully planned progression from the ages of five to sixteen or eighteen.

This was not the case everywhere. When local authorities had reorganised schools in the late '60s and early '70s, a number had chosen to introduce middle schools. Since then most of these had reverted to a two-tier system with transfer at the traditional age of eleven. Bradford, with its 9-13 middle schools, remained one of the few three-tier authorities in the country and, increasingly from the mid-1990s, questions were being asked as to whether it too should review its provision. Two related issues drove the debate. The first was to do with standards. Bradford had, for some time, been a low-performing Authority in terms of national figures. There were various reasons why this was the case but it was suggested that one cause could be that some middle schools were under-performing and that in any case two transfers in four years disrupted pupil progress. Moreover, the Ilkley Pyramid was an exception. In Bradford the situation was much more fluid and a lot of middle and, especially, upper schools drew from so many feeder schools that meaningful liaison was impossible. The second issue was financial. An authority with three tiers had more small schools than one with two tiers. These were seen as less cost-effective than larger schools and, in an authority which was endemically impoverished, it was important to make the best use of limited resources.

The possibility of change had been in the air for several years without ever being taken seriously. The first intimation that something more fundamental was afoot came in 1997. The Head reported to Governors in September:

The major policy thrust at local level is the review of school provision launched by the LEA in May. It is intended that the review will look at concerns that current educational, financial and social issues stem at least in part from the pattern of schools across the district. It will also look at possible alternatives to the present three-phase structure and propose a programme of change. It seems at this stage unlikely that the status quo will continue. It is less clear what might be the alternative arrangements and the time scale over which they might be introduced.

The consultation was a massive exercise, as an avalanche of meetings was launched throughout Bradford and district. They were mainly for parents and governors, though other members of the community, including some teachers, also attended. Those in the Ilkley area were not happy affairs. Parents liked their local schools. They were successful and the current arrangement worked well for their children. "If it ain't broke, don't fix it" was the oft-repeated mantra. There was also a feeling that the consultation was a sham, that the political decision had already been taken and that the meetings were simply an uncomfortable necessity. This may have been the case in some areas. That it was not necessarily so in Ilkley was demonstrated when the Authority, aware of the strength of local feeling, put the ball back into the schools' court and offered to allow the Ilkley three-tier system to remain intact.

Although this had superficial attractions and may, for some, have been the preferred solution, the reality was more complex. While the loudest voices were against change, there was a

Cheques for almost £2,700 for Children in Need are presented to TV Newsreader Sophie Raworth in 1997.

Andrew Lambert.

significant body of opinion which favoured a two-tier arrangement. There was no argument about the high quality of the local middle schools, nor with the idea that for some children it might be helpful to have an intermediate stage between primary and secondary. But there was an equally strongly-held view that many children were ready for the challenges of secondary schooling at eleven and would benefit from three years of secondary education prior to commencing GCSE courses. It was also generally agreed that there were important advantages in aligning the age of transfer with a key stage division and that, in a world where middle schools were already an endangered species, to retain an island of three-tier provision within a two-tier Authority made no sense educationally or administratively.

In February 1998 John Cockshott, the Chairman of Governors, reported:

> The Governing Body has looked closely at all the options presented for consideration in the Review of Schools Interim Report. We have considered the effect of each option on this school and on the Ilkley Pyramid of Schools as a whole. We are recommending to Bradford LEA that it adopts the principle of two-phase education.

The final decision wasn't long coming. The outcome of the Authority's Review was reported by the Head and Chairman:

Chairman of Governors John Cockshott presents certificates to Year 11 students at the Craiglands in November 1999.

Andrew Lambert.

The Year 9 Residential 1998. l to r:

Gillian Robertson, Georgina Wood, Aimee Coltman, Danielle Jones.

Andrew Lambert.

The result will be that Bradford will come into line with the majority of the rest of the country and have a two phase education system, with a break between the primary and secondary phases at the age of eleven. The proposal for this school is that, retaining its present title, it will become a secondary school catering for pupils from the ages of 11 to 18. The preferred option is that, with the support of a building programme, the School should operate on the present site.

The question of the name was again the subject of vigorous debate. In the end the Governors felt that continuity was as important as change and, as thirty years earlier, that a name which had been rooted in the community for almost four hundred years should be retained. The question of the site was a different matter. For years the building had been crowded. Specialist teaching accommodation was at a premium and had only remained viable through the addition of temporary rooms. Relative to newly-designed schools, the overall site area was limited. It was a matter of concern as to whether an additional five hundred children and fifty or more staff could be accommodated safely and comfortably. The problem was that no one could come up with a suitable alternative; of the two mentioned, a move to Ilkley College (yet again) was considered impractical and the Ilkley

Middle School site was too small. The option of a permanent split site was considered and quickly dismissed. The Local Authority said that, on the basis of national templates, the Cowpasture Road site was of an appropriate size and that in any case there was insufficient money for a complete re-build. It was finally agreed that, with carefully designed new accommodation and a sympathetic use of the land available, continued use of the existing site was the only practical way forward.

Meanwhile a Labour government had been elected in 1997, with "Education, Education, Education" famously at the top of its agenda. Its reforming zeal was soon apparent. By the autumn two bills were on their way through Parliament. They made local authorities accountable in the same way as schools and prioritised such areas as the student loans scheme, vocational education and professional development. A General Teaching Council was created and mandatory qualifications for headteachers were introduced. This was only a start. Over the next ten years schools were increasingly to feel the mailed fist of government as it sought to drive up standards.

On the verge of all this uncertainty, the 1998 exam results were

Pupils walk to the Sports Hall in September 1999 for an assembly at the start of the school year.

The picture shows the 1971 extensions to the north of the school. Beyond the trees on the right are the tennis courts, soon to become the site for the 2003 extensions.

the best-ever. In the same year the tennis team progressed, for the second year running, to the national finals, making them one of the country's top twelve teams. The Under 14 and 15 hockey teams were undefeated. The Under 18 team were Bradford champions. Four boys, Jon Birtwhistle, Matthew Dorrill, Simon Tweddle and Richard Airy represented Bradford at soccer. Andrew Souyave won the Best Speaker Award in the Daniel Nelstrop Debating Competition. The Young Engineers team of Alice Campbell, Kristen McKeown and Hazel Acomb not only competed in the national finals but won three prizes, including first in their class. The Children in Need Appeal raised £1,337. Twenty sixth formers visited China. Twenty one pupils trained to be anti-bullying counsellors. Mark Roberts and David Zezulka, two sixth formers, produced 'Our Town' with a cast from Years Nine and Ten. The Newsletter listed over forty weekly extra-curricular activities. Almost a hundred students went on to Higher Education. Nor was the past forgotten. Although the Old Olicanians' Association had long ceased, former pupils still kept in touch and throughout the 1990s reunions became increasingly popular. In 1997 alone there were three, one from the 1960s, one from the 1980s and one from the class of 1947. This last was particularly well-attended, with Old Olicanians travelling from as far afield as Canada, South Africa and New Zealand as well as various corners of the U.K. The reception at the Craiglands, where the address was given by the Bishop of Durham, was a convivial and hugely enjoyable occasion.

From September 2000 the School once again took pupils from the age of eleven. These Year 8 pupils wrote for the March 2002 edition of the School Newsletter from which this picture is taken.

Back, left to right: Kirtsy Dwyer, Amanda Thompson, Chris Harvey, Jimmy Macpherson Front, left to right: Lawrence Yates, Matthew Thornton, Michael Seed.

The financial situation had begun to stabilise. The School continued to run a significant deficit and, if the position did not improve, nor did it deteriorate. In 1998 the new Secretary of State, David Blunkett, claimed to have put £1bn of additional funding into education, with a strong recommendation that it should find its way into schools. Bradford's share was around £9.5m but virtually all of it was required to enable the Authority's budget to roll on at its current level. Indeed it was estimated that a further £5m would be needed to enable its schools to balance their budgets. In 2000 there was the first really positive news for many years when, in addition to the Authority indicating it would give the secondary sector the bulk of any additional funding, the School was given £50,000 as its share of a one-off direct payment by the Government.

Inevitably the Schools' Reorganisation continued to hold centre stage. By mid-1998 it was clear that September 2000 would be the start date. It was also clear that the new buildings would not be ready before 2001 and that, for the second time in thirty years, there would have to be a split site. The School wanted any new build to be on land at the lower part of the site and, once an architect had been appointed, plans for this were drawn. There remained a suspicion, however, that an extension on the area of the tennis courts would commend itself as a cheaper option. It was a suspicion not entirely allayed by the assurances of Bradford's Principal Buildings Officer in late 1999 that "the tennis court option is dead in the water."

There were other matters to address. Teachers, many of whom had given the bulk of their careers to middle school children, suddenly had to choose between working in primary or secondary. In Bradford itself the situation was extremely complicated. In Ilkley, Addingham and Burley, though there were difficulties and some personal disappointments, the pyramid structure eased the

'The Threepenny Opera' - March 1999.

Supporting charities has always been important for the School. Here, in November 2001, lower School pupils Georgie Hallam, Will Lambert and Zosha Allen carry some of the four hundred shoeboxes containing dried produce which were destined for orphanages in Romania.

Photograph from the School Newsletter.

process and most who wished to remain in the area were able to do so. There was also the question of resources. Somehow an equitable distribution from the closing middle schools had to be arranged. It too was a complex business. It was rumoured that during the summer holiday of 2000 every serviceable pantechnicon in the Bradford area had been booked and was plying its trade twenty-four hours a day. Finally, Ilkley Middle School, as the only building which could serve as the twin site, had to undergo building work. After briefly considering it as a Sixth Form Centre, it was decided that it would be occupied by Years Seven and Eight.

In the middle of all this, the Government produced a Green Paper, aptly titled 'Teachers – Meeting the Challenge of Change'. It represented an attempt to reform the structure of the profession and it made clear the direction the Government wanted to take. There were to be extended pay scales, new appraisal arrangements, Advanced Skills Teachers and fast-tracking and training for heads. Although implementation of some proposals was deferred, this remained a major thrust of Government policy into the new millennium. A significant re-organisation of post-16 education was also announced, with the introduction in September 2000 of AS levels. These provided recognition for Year Twelve work and, because they usually entailed an extra subject, helped to broaden the curriculum. However they also increased student workload and hence reduced time for extra-curricular activities.

The old 13-18 Upper School bade farewell with record results, an 'A' level pass rate of almost 95% and a GCSE 5 A*-C figure of over 74%. Bradford became one of the authorities included in the Government's 'Excellence in Cities' scheme and, although the majority of the funding went to inner-city schools, Ilkley was able to benefit from the 'Gifted and Talented' programme and set about identifying an appropriate cohort of pupils. An exhibition of the School's art work, appropriately called 'Transition', was mounted for three weeks at The Manor House and the musical 'Annie', produced and directed by Kathy McLelland, with musical direction by Keiron Anderson, played to full houses. Two A Level Art students, Katy Wright and Tom Anderson designed mosaics, constructed from pebbles from the river, for the Darwin Millennium Garden at the top of Wells Road. There was a sixth form trip to India and work experience in Gerona for A Level Spanish students. The PTA staged 'An Evening with Alan Titchmarsh' at the King's Hall which was a sell-out.

The accommodation issue was settled when it became clear that the Local Authority was not prepared to consider any option other than building on the tennis courts. The School was told bluntly that if it refused then it would simply remain on a split-site. A contractor, Bovis Lend Lease, was appointed and the lengthy planning process began. As funding and building deadlines slipped, it also became clear that split-site working might extend beyond one year. In the meantime Ilkley Middle School, soon to become Ilkley Grammar Lower School, was being adapted, with the addition of two new Science laboratories, a Technology room, five temporary classrooms and disabled access.

The new 11-18 Ilkley Grammar School opened on 6th September 2000. In spite of extra preparation days at either end of the summer holiday, it was a close-run thing. With three weeks to go, the hall at Valley Drive was piled with a mountain of furniture and equipment drawn from closing middle schools. It was only through superhuman efforts by Richard Jennings, Head of Ilkley Middle School, who became Head of Lower School, and other staff that everything was ready in time. Some teachers were busy until late on the last evening, while laboratory fittings were finally completed at 3am. As the Head reported:

> The transformation in a matter of weeks from a building site and resource depository into a working school was little short of miraculous. Most teaching areas were well-ordered, clean and attractively presented. Most remarkable of all, it was possible to hold an assembly on the first morning. It was not only a significant occasion; it was a moving one in that it represented the culmination of so much effort and

The Under 16 Football Team 2001-02, winners of the Airedale and Wharfedale Cup.

Back Row l to r: Henry Wood, Nick Sugden, Richard Sharpe, Robert Tankard, Richard Duke, Ben Naylor, Elliot Exley.

Front Row l to r: Jim Hunter,, Adam Davey, Andrew Driver, Stuart Baker, Matthew Tosh.

dedication. A great deal of progress has been made since then, to the extent that after only two weeks we were able to hold another assembly with an orchestra and readings at which the Director of Education and the Chair of Governors were our guests.

So, for the second time in thirty years, the School had to adapt to life on a split site and everyone had to get used to new ways of working. Staff were encouraged to teach unfamiliar year groups, even though this meant more travelling. A school mini bus was pressed into service and plied a regular route along Bolling Road. Its driver, Mick Wild, revealed in the Newsletter that, as well as carrying people, he had also transported machinery, shopping, internal mail, clay models and, on one memorable day, a deer's head. Travel periods had to be built into what became a more complicated timetable. Opportunities were taken, through extra-curricular activities, to enable pupils from the two sites to work together, but they were necessarily limited. Nevertheless by February 2001 the Head was reporting on "the remarkable progress made. There is a great deal of evidence for this: the greater staff cohesiveness across both the staffroom as a whole and in subject and year teams, the impressive list of activities, the quality of work being produced, the developing links throughout the community, the impressive 'set piece' productions and events." These included a Christmas Music and Drama Evening with pupils from Year 7 to Year 13, drawn from two buildings over a mile apart and produced by teachers who, three months earlier, had scarcely known each other.

There were other developments. John Cockshott who, as Chairman of Governors, had helped to guide the School through major changes, retired and was succeeded by Michael Noble. There was a new uniform, with blazers and a different-coloured tie for each year group. The Ilkley Pyramid, which had served the area for many years, had now lost a layer and, in a more egalitarian spirit, was re-named the Wharfe Valley Partnership. There were now five primary schools. Those in Addingham and Burley occupied the former middle school buildings. The three in Ilkley were in the former first schools of All Saints (which moved to a long-awaited new building in 2002), Ashlands and Bolling Road (re-named Ben Rhydding Primary). The Partnership provided a forum for Heads, individually and with Chairs of Governors, to share experience and plan jointly. A national system of

Blazers were re-introduced when the School became 11-18. Each year group up to Year 11 wears a different-coloured tie.

Performance Management for teachers was introduced; all teachers had to be issued with job descriptions and set performance targets. In the run-up to reorganisation Bradford Authority had its own Ofsted inspection. In the subsequent report, published in May 2000, it was roundly criticised. It was judged that the Authority was not performing well and was providing schools with a poor level of service. Poor leadership, both political and professional was highlighted. As a result it was decided that the majority of services should be externally provided and Education Bradford, with a private service provider SERCO, was set up to manage them.

Meanwhile building negotiations dragged on. The Authority had a template of the rooms required for a given number of pupils. This became the subject of hard bargaining between the School and Bovis, with the involvement of Bradford Chief Executive, Ian Stewart. By May 2001 plans had been developed and the Head reported, "We all remain wedded to the goal of establishing the school on one site in September 2002." Work was planned to start in the autumn. That was postponed to January 2002, then to February, then to March, then to April. Four classrooms, occupied by the Languages Department, sprouted on the front lawn and two more next to Springs Lane. Building work began on 26th June, with 15th August 2003 as the scheduled completion date. The split site arrangement was to last not, as originally planned, for one year, but for three.

Self-help was still important. The pavilion, so proudly unveiled in 1963, was beginning to show its age. Restoration work began in 2001, costing almost £40,000, with generous donations from the Friends of IGS and the PTA plus a budgeted sum and matched government and local authority funding. When the Sixth Form Centre needed refurbishing, Year 13 student Sarah Hardcastle got to work and, by applying for grants, raised £4,000. The faded walls were given a new lick of (donated) paint in cheerful reds and yellows, 1970s curtains were replaced, some chairs were renewed and others re-covered.

In April 2001 the School was shocked at the sudden death of Andrew Lambert. He had joined the staff in 1968, becoming Head of Physics and Head of Science. As the tribute in the Newsletter said, "To have been taught by Andrew Lambert was a privilege. When he was with a class he was doing what he enjoyed most, he was doing what he did best and he was very, very good at it." Less than a year later Peter Burton, the Head of Geography, another enormously gifted teacher, died after a long illness.

Andrew Lambert, who taught at the Grammar School from 1968 until his sudden death in 2001. As well as being Head of Physics and Head of Science, he took countless photos of school activities throughout the 1980s and 90s.

Oliver Louden, an A Level student wrote, "He was very highly respected among all the students he taught. He will be greatly missed and the memory of him will always remain with me." He is commemorated in an annual award for A Level Geography.

The Newsletter, now in glossy format, continued to chronicle school life. Eleanor Kitchen, new to the school in 2001, showed that little had changed in terms of 'First Impressions':

Head of Geography Peter Burton who died in 2001

> I spent the last three weeks of the summer term thinking about my new school. Unfortunately I encountered my first problem of the BIG DAY only thirty seconds after leaving my home. Cycling in a wrap-round skirt is not a good idea! However, on arriving at the great hall on the Lower School site, flushed with excitement, I soon forgot my embarrassing travel arrangements as off I was led through a maze of corridors to my classroom. I think Ilkley Grammar School is a palace. The clubs are great, things are well organised, the dinners are great and the staff are lovely. All in all, I think I'm going to enjoy life here and I hope to bring the school some success with cross country running and not cause too much grief.

Hilary Walkley, the Upper School Receptionist, saw things slightly differently:

> Keys for car servicing, dinner money dropped off to prevent malnutrition, deliveries of homework to ward off detentions, all are easily handled without worrying the Health and Safety Executive. There is a feeling of well-being in looking after something as British as a cricket bat but the remnants of a long-finished rugby game are less desirable. Unsavoury bags appear like mushrooms, to be found in the early morning. The aroma of the games exertions and the herbage gathered from the bottom of the scrum send my nose in an upward direction and my hands itch for the comfort of Marigolds. Lost property is an enigma; property found never quite matches property lost. Typically, a dental brace was handed in the day before a set of false teeth were lost at the car boot sale. Close, but hardly a fair exchange. Oh, and if any one sees a young man in blazer and underpants – I have his trousers.

By May 2002 there were even signs of financial optimism. The deficit was now under control and there were indications of improvements in funding. The Head's report to Governors suggested the deficit might be reduced significantly over the next three to four years. There were two incentives. Firstly it was clear that Education Bradford was not as lenient nor as inefficient as the old LEA and was keen to work with the School on a robust recovery plan. Secondly any such plan would be a necessary accompaniment to an application for Specialist School status. Already three Bradford schools had been chosen for an accelerated bid. Five more were yet to be chosen but it appeared inner city bids would be favoured and therefore that the School would need to make a separate application.

Ofsted came calling again in April 2002. By now the format had changed. Instead of an interminable period of preparation, schools were given only a few weeks' notice. Those giving no cause for concern had a two-day 'light touch' inspection in Years 7-11, though the Sixth Form was looked at over a full week. The inspection model now looked more closely at a school's ability accurately to monitor its own progress. Hence (apart from the Sixth From) there was less emphasis on lesson observation and more on the quality of the School's self-assessment. The report, published in June, began:

> Ilkley Grammar School is a very effective school. Pupils' attainment is high. Results in external examinations both at 16 and in the Sixth Form, are well above the national average, and have continued to improve since the last inspection. Teaching is of a high standard throughout the school. The Headteacher and senior staff provide clear educational direction. The management of pupils and of the learning process is very effective. The school provides good value for money.

It went on to refer to the "high expectations of pupils; their attainment is well above the national average and above average for similar schools." Their "behaviour and attitudes to learning are very good; they come to school to work." The report also commented on relationships which are "very good at all levels. There is an equal partnership in learning which contributes strongly to the standards achieved." For all associated with the School it was a very pleasing report, especially since it was particularly complimentary about the way the reorganisation had been handled.

As far back as September 2001, Peter Wood had indicated that he would be retiring in July 2002, by which time, it had been

assumed, the building work would have been completed. In the event it had barely begun. Gillian James, Headteacher at Archbishop Temple School, Preston was appointed to the post, the tenth Head since 1893 and the first female. It fell to her to oversee the return to one site. Once again Ilkley Grammar School would be resuming its traditional role – a secondary school based entirely at Cowpasture Road.

The Swimming Pool, opened in 1913, is still being used in the twenty-first century.

A Specialist School

Not least of the challenges facing the new Head was the task of running a school on two sites while preparing for life on one, and at the same time managing major building work. By January 2003 the tennis courts had disappeared, and, though the view was a muddy expanse, pile-driving was complete. Gradually the new 35 room teaching block took shape so that, by June, although the roof was still unfinished, internal fittings and decoration were well advanced. Unsurprisingly, in spite of everything apparently being on course and the new term scheduled to start two weeks late, it all came down to the wire. The problem wasn't with the new building, which was delivered on time, but the old one, which, as Mrs James reported, required modification:

Gillian James, Headteacher since 2002.

The very significant works in the old building presented the serious challenges we had expected – and more: unforeseen asbestos, for example. Despite our early, and well-founded warnings to Bradford, the contractors caused us major headaches in terms of delivery and had domino effects on other contractors waiting to fit laboratory furniture. We kept the pressure on, and stepped it up in the closing stages. Against the odds, and with our staff's joinery skills and bitten tongues, we welcomed our students at 8.30 am on Tuesday 16th September.

It was a significant moment. For the first time in three years the School was on one site. For the first time in over thirty years it was an 11-18 secondary school. For the first time in its history, certainly since 1893, it welcomed not one but three new year groups to Cowpasture Road.

There were other pressing matters. With over half of England's secondary schools having achieved specialist status, the Head and Governors were now keen to take forward an application. A prerequisite for the bid was that the School should be able to attract £50,000 in sponsorship but, in spite of a lot of hard work, the response from the local business community failed to match that figure. The day was saved by a substantial anonymous donation from an Ilkley resident and by March 2004 the Head was able to report that the money had been raised. At the same time the budget situation was improving thanks to various economies, including a reduction from two Deputy Heads to one, and a Leadership Incentive Grant of £130,000 a year for three years as

The new building, which opened in September 2003 on the site of the old tennis courts.

Team Challenge students pictured at Ingleborough Hall.

part of Bradford's Excellence in Cities status, so that by the end of the year the overall deficit had been halved.

Another feature of Excellence in Cities, the Gifted and Talented programme, continued to develop. One regular activity was the Team Challenge. This began in 2002 with a three-day residential at Ingleborough Hall for sixty four Year 7 and 8 pupils, led by sixteen Year 12 students, and has since continued on an annual basis. Ingleborough was also used each year for intensive rehearsals for the regular musical productions written and directed by Kathy McLelland and Keiron Anderson. In 2003 another annual event, the Presentation Evening, returned to the King's Hall. There was plenty to celebrate, with a 99% pass rate at A Level and 73% gaining 5 or more A*-C grades at GCSE. As always there were staff changes; in 2004 three long-serving teachers retired: Maureen Shackleton, who had been a Deputy Head since 1987, Ken Gibson who had been appointed to the P.E. Department in 1971, subsequently becoming Head of Careers, and Keith Hodgson, Head of Sociology and Psychology, who had begun teaching in Ilkley in 1973. Events much further back in the School's history were commemorated in May 2004 when forty Year 9 pupils travelled to Belgium to visit battlefields and memorials of the First World War. It was a particularly poignant trip as they searched for the names of fallen Old Olicanians. They were able to find five at the Menin Gate and a further four (including Eric Wilkinson) at Tyne Cot Cemetery. Other foreign visits were afoot, from the Coutances Exchange, still going strong after almost sixty years, to a more exotic expedition to Tanzania by fifteen sixth formers who, with money they had already raised, helped to refurbish a primary school building in Shirimatunda. Closer to home, musicians from the School were among the group which welcomed and played for the VIP party which came to Ilkley in February 2004 to celebrate the 50th anniversary of the Yorkshire Dales National Park; Sir Jimmy Savile and actor Brian Blessed were kept busy signing autographs.

The School made its first bid for Specialist Status in March 2004. This was not successful but comfort was taken from the fact that few schools were able to succeed first time round. It was encouraged by positive feedback to re-submit, which it did in October. In January 2005 it was announced that the bid had been successful and so, from September 2005 the School was re-designated as a Specialist School in Science and Humanities, with a focus on the core subjects, English, Maths and Science. One of the benefits of the new status was an injection of further and recurrent funding, which not only gave the School the additional information technology it needed but helped to ensure that the deficit was wiped out and that, for the first time for many years, it was able to balance its books.

The unprecedented waves of educational change and intervention continued unabated, as the Department for Education (DfE) became the DfES (Department for Education and Skills) and then, in 2007, the DCSF (Department for Children, Schools and Families). The Workforce Remodelling Agreement came into force in September 2003, starting with the twenty four tasks teachers should no longer be required to do, followed by absence cover restrictions, a ban on teachers invigilating exams and dedicated PPA (Planning, Preparation and Assessment) time. The thrust of much of this legislation was an attempt to ensure that teachers were freed from extraneous responsibilities and were able to devote their energies to teaching. However lack of government funding meant that the School faced considerable challenges in recruiting the extra support staff to deliver the agreement. In 2006 mandatory staff restructuring was introduced, with Teaching and Learning Responsibilities replacing Management Allowances. There was a national review of the 14-19 curriculum, which heralded the birth of vocational diplomas but not the death of the 'gold standard' A Level. Extended Schools were followed by Sustainable Schools. The ECM (Every Child Matters) agenda permeated all schools' work and food standards also appeared on a crowded centre stage. Schools were becoming ever more accountable and increasingly responsible for their own self-evaluation and self-monitoring. Ilkley Grammar was not alone in acquiring an SIO (School Improvement Officer) and an SIP (School Improvement Partner) as well as having to manage the revised (once again) Performance Management regulations.

There was change locally as well. As a result of SERCO's take-over of Bradford's education services, the School found itself in one of six Confederations – the Three Valleys – alongside Greenhead, Oakbank and Holy Family from Keighley, Parkside in Cullingworth and Bingley, a grouping which almost exactly mirrored the Consortium arrangement of twenty years earlier. Bradford was also a 'pathfinder authority' for the government's 'Building Schools for the Future' initiative.

The Newsletter, expanded and increasingly professional thanks to developing technology, continues to chronicle the many facets of school life. Exam results have maintained their improvement, with the best-ever results at A Level in 2006 and at GCSE in 2007. During the winter of 2004-05 there were thirty five games teams. The McLelland – Anderson musicals (most recently 'Live at the Empire' and 'School – The Scandal') have become an annual fixture. There were summer World Challenge trips to Namibia and, in 2006, to Thailand and Cambodia. There were visits to

The World Challenge team, led by Jeff Pancott, visits Thailand and Cambodia during summer 2006.

Iceland and New York and, in October 2006, a cricket tour to Barbados. Sixth Form numbers continued to increase until they exceeded three hundred. A school minibus able to accommodate the four wheelchair students was provided by the PTA. Six PTA Car Boot Sales in 2005 raised over £13,000. A Positive Behaviour initiative was introduced in 2005. Healthy eating became an important focus for school meals. 2007 saw the sixtieth anniversary of the Coutances exchange, though, sadly, Georges Lechaptois died in 2002. Students in Years 7-11 worked with local artist Jo Whitehead. The PTA resurrected its May Ball. These and many other stories pop up from a cursory trawl through recent Newsletters but they represent an enormous variety of articles,

The Entrance Hall has changed little in over a hundred years.

reports and features which are testimony to the richness of the School's life in the 21st Century.

As always, the Newsletters include staff changes and in 2006 three long-serving teachers retired: Ian Gasper, who had been Deputy Head since 1989, who had led the application for Specialist Status and who was succeeded by Adam Daly, Sue Robins, Head of Modern Languages, and John Wright, who had helped to pioneer Information Technology. There was another change in 2006, this time to the crest. The coats of arms of the Whitton and Watkinson families were retained but the whole thing was simplified by removing the Whitton owl (ducally gorged) and also the foliage around the crest, known irreverently as "the cabbage leaves".

All of which brings us to 2007, the 400th year of Ilkley Grammar School. It began inauspiciously with one of the huge new roof cowlings blowing off in a gale, resulting in the site being closed or partially closed for several days. The anniversary celebrations were launched in February, with the visit of HRH The Princess Royal, Princess Anne, following in the footsteps of her

Princess Anne visits the School in February 2007.

predecessor, Princess Mary, who had opened the building extensions forty three years earlier. It was a day to remember, with twenty police officers with dogs arriving at 8am, five and a half hours before the Princess landed by helicopter on the school field and took a motorcade to the front entrance. There she was greeted by a samba band, the School Council, the History Club, the Head, Ros Beeson the Chair of Governors and the Mayor and Mayoress of Bradford. She was "a very easy and relaxed guest, engaging with students and staff, interested in the School's history and vision and willingly following in her great aunt's footsteps." At the same time 'School – The Scandal' began its run. Set in a school also celebrating its 400th anniversary, it looked back over its history and into the future.

There were other celebrations. The 'Class of '47' held a reunion in September (they meet every ten years) and their fond memories are testament to the lasting impact of the School. Others endorse this. Memories from those visiting for the Community Open Day included this from Janet Hollis (née Eley) who attended from 1960-66, in Mr Walbank's time: "Discipline. Uniform. Beautiful building and grounds. Understanding staff. Friendly peers. Thank you for six very happy years and the best education I could ever have asked for." There was a summer concert in July, a performance of 'Twelfth Night' in December, an Anniversary Ball,

School reunions have become increasingly popular. This group from 1947 were re-acquainted with each other and the School in September 2007.

a Thanksgiving Service at St Margaret's, where Mr Atkinson's memorial plaque still stands, and a display of some of the archive in the Library. Dr C. L. Davidson, the most senior Old Olicanian, was interviewed for the Newsletter by two sixth formers, Mark Coldwell and Sam Brown. He was a pupil from 1918 to 1923, in the early days of Mr Frazer:

> I was eight years old when I started school here. I boarded for my first term. I found boarding awful. I found that we were hungry all the time. We had a rota of who got the extra sandwich. One thing I do remember was the quality of the jam we were given while boarding. It was delicious but we could have done with more. My favourite teacher was Mr Ebdon; he made French very enjoyable. My least favourite was Mr Frazer. He was a particularly stern man. He was a good teacher, but very strict. He would make you stand on your desk in assembly, should you have done anything wrong. We were all fearful of this. The humiliation was horrific. Personally I was caned twice, most likely for pushing the teachers too far with my cheek. The Head Boy was Barratt and he was my friend. He died and the following term another student caught pneumonia and died, so it was a very low time in school. I used to love skating on the tarn in winter, and when it snowed the teachers would let us sledge down Cowpasture Road – that was very enjoyable. I also enjoyed being taught by such great teachers.

There was one more significant event in 2007 – an Ofsted inspection in May, the first for five years, followed by another excellent report, which began:

> Students, parents, teachers and inspectors all agree that Ilkley Grammar School is a good school. Not only that, it has some aspects that are outstanding, not least the superb way in which students are cared for, and their personal development and well-being enhanced.

It went on to say that "students are proud of their school. They behave excellently in lessons and around the building . . . Students learn well because their teachers are extremely knowledgeable about their subjects . . . Relationships are excellent and are founded on mutual trust and respect . . . The Headteacher and her deputy have a crystal clear vision for the school . . . Consequently the school shows a good capacity to improve further."

*Gillian James
with students
and the 2007
Ofsted Report.*

Thus, with a final flourish and a glimpse into the future, is completed the story of four hundred years of education in the Grammar School at Ilkley. It is a story of continual change and development. It is a story of challenges, of commitment and achievement. But above all, it is a story of people, from those in the early 1600s who were determined that a school should be established to those who will take it forward in the 21st century. It is a story of the countless thousands of girls and boys who have been educated there, of all the dedicated men and women who have worked there across the years and of those local people who have taken on the responsibility of governance. It is a story that is in train, a work that is in progress and it is a school of which, as it enters its fifth century, its founding fathers would be proud.

Sources

Bibliography

Denton's Ilkley Directory, Guide Book and Almanac (1871).

Shuttleworth's Guide to Ilkley (1884).

Robert Collyer and J. Horsfall Turner:
Ilkley Ancient and Modern (1885).

Norman Salmon: Ilkley Grammar School 1607 – 1957 (1957).

Curtis and Boultwood:
An Introductory History of English Education Since 1800 (1966).

John Le Patourel: Ilkley Parish Church (1968).

Ilkley National Schools and All Saints School 1872 – 1972 (1972).

Don Mosey:
We Don't Play It For Fun: A Story Of Yorkshire Cricket (1988).

Tony Barringer: Ilkley Grammar School: A Century at School (1993).

Margaret and Denis Warwick: Our Schools – A History of Schools in Burley-in-Wharfedale (1998).

Mike Dixon: Ilkley: History and Guide (2002).

Nikolaus Pevsner:
The Buildings of England: Yorkshire: The West Riding (2003).

West Yorkshire Archive

Leeds Archive: The Weston Papers (previously held at Weston Hall and donated to the County Archive in 1973).

Bradford Archive: Governing Body Minutes 1938 - 1943.

Ilkley Grammar School Archive

Letters of the Clerk to the Governors (1872-1886).

Return and Digest of Endowed Charities (West Riding of York): Parish of Ilkley (1894).

Letters of Frederic Swann (1897-1904).

The Olicanian (1900 - 1971).

The Old Olicanian (1902 - 1964).

John W. Dixon: Outline History of Governors (1931).

Ilkley Secondary School Log Book (1950 - 1970).

The School Newsletter (1993 – 2007).

Extracts from the Ilkley Gazette, the Ilkley Free Press, the Yorkshire Post.

Various Governing Body Minutes.

Various Legal Documents, Account Books, Reports, Letters, Illustrations and Photographs.

[handwritten:] Glaring omission in death of Mr Bilsby

[handwritten:] I was There :

[handwritten:] October 1966 — Christmas 1970

[handwritten:] Nov 20 1971 married Mick Pinder.